CW00468305

__Introduction__

This book explores the five classes of the one phylum of vertebrates: mammals, birds, fish, reptiles and amphibians.

Mammals have hair/fur and nurse their young. Birds have wings and feathers for flight. Fish are aquatic with over 30,000 known species. Reptiles have adapted to harsh environments, and amphibians can live on land and in water.

Vertebrates are a diverse group of animals. Each class has its own unique characteristics and adaptations that have allowed them to thrive in their respective environments.

A book that contains 100 facts about each class of vertebrates would be a fascinating and informative read for anyone interested in the animal kingdom.

Whether you are a student or a naturalist, this book offers a comprehensive and exciting look into the world of vertebrates.

5 Classes

1- Mammals

1. Mammals are warm-blooded animals. They can regulate their body temperature internally, which allows them to live in a variety of environments.

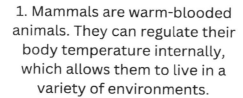

2. Mammals are characterized by the presence of mammary glands that produce milk to nourish their young.

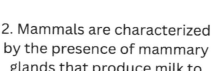

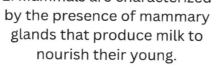

3. There are over 5,400 species of mammals on Earth. Mammals have been around for approximately 200 million years, with the earliest known mammalian ancestors appearing during the Late Triassic period.

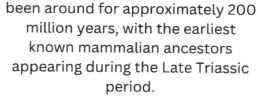

1

4. The largest mammal is the blue whale, which can weigh up to 200 tons (181,437 kg).

5. The smallest mammal is the bumblebee bat, which weighs less than a penny.

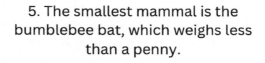

6. The longest-living mammal is the bowhead whale, which can live up to 200 years.

7. The smallest mammal brain belongs to the Etruscan shrew, which weighs only 0.1 grams.

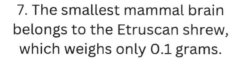

---

8. The biggest mammal brain belongs to the sperm whale, which weighs about 18 pounds.

---

9. Raccoons are known carriers of diseases such as rabies, so it's important to avoid contact with them in the wild.

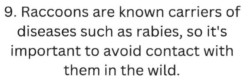

3

10. Most mammals give birth to live young, but a few species lay eggs. The platypus is one of the few mammals that lay eggs.

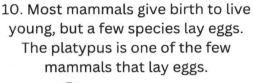

---

11. The kangaroo and its relatives, including wallabies and tree kangaroos, are the only mammals that hop.

---

12. Bats are the only mammals that can fly.

13. The sloth moves so slowly that algae often grows on its fur.

---

14. The echidna and platypus are the only mammals that lay eggs and produce milk.

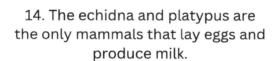

---

15. The cheetah is the fastest land mammal, reaching speeds of up to 70 miles (112.65 kilometres) per hour.

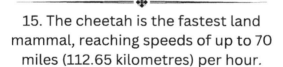

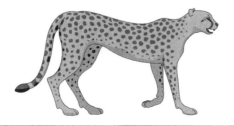

5

16. The elephant has the longest gestation period of any mammal, at 22 months.

17. Humpback whales are known for their complex songs, which can last up to 20 minutes.

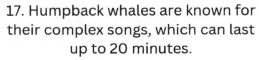

18. A group of otters is called a romp.

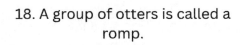

6

19. A group of bats is called a colony.

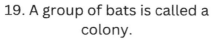

20. A group of kangaroos is called a mob.

21. A group of elephants is called a herd.

7

22. A group of lions is called a pride.

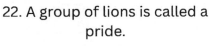

23. A group of gorillas is called a troop.

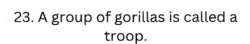

24. A group of whales is called a pod.

8

25. Mammals have three main types of teeth: incisors, canines, and molars.
They also have a diaphragm, a muscle that helps them breathe.

26. Hippos are known for their aggressive behavior, particularly towards humans who may accidentally come too close to them while they are in the water or on land.

27. Hamsters are small rodents that are native to Syria, but they are now kept as pets all around the world.
They have very poor eyesight.

28. Dolphins are highly intelligent marine mammals that belong to the family Delphinidae, which includes over 90 species of dolphins, whales, and porpoises. They use a form of echolocation to navigate and find prey, sending out high-pitched clicks and listening for the echoes to bounce back.

29. The red kangaroo is the largest marsupial in the world. They can jump up to three times their own body length in one leap.

30. Marsupials are mammals that carry their young in a pouch.

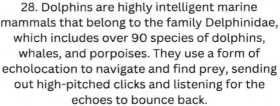

31. The koala feeds almost exclusively on eucalyptus leaves.

32. The platypus has a duck-like bill and webbed feet, but is a mammal, not a bird.

33. The elephant's trunk is a specialized nose and upper lip that is used for breathing, smelling, and grasping objects.

34. The giant panda has a thumb-like structure on its front paws that helps it grasp bamboo shoots

---

35. The giraffe has the longest neck of any mammal, with up to seven vertebrae elongated.

---

36. The African elephant is the largest land animal in the world, weighing up to 14,000 pounds (6,350 kg) and standing up to 13 feet (4 meters) tall at the shoulder.

37. The polar bear is the largest land predator in the world, weighing up to 1,500 pounds (680 kilos).

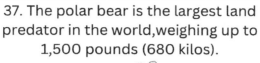

38. The blue whale has a heart that can weigh as much as a car and is the largest heart of any animal.

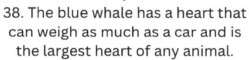

39. The Tasmanian devil is a carnivorous marsupial native to Australia.

13

40. The kangaroo rat is able to survive without water, obtaining moisture from its food.

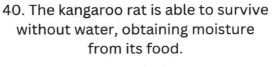

41. The armadillo has a hard, bony shell covering its body.

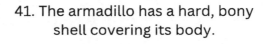

42. The meerkat is a small mammal that lives in large groups called clans.

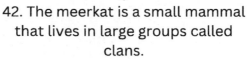

43. The bison is a large, herbivorous mammal native to North America.

---

44. The common house mouse has a lifespan of about 2 years.

---

45. The hippopotamus (hippos) is one of the deadliest animals in Africa, responsible for more human deaths than any other large animal.

15

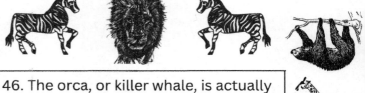

46. The orca, or killer whale, is actually a type of dolphin.

47. The rhinoceros has thick, protective skin and a large horn on its nose. The horn is made of keratin, the same material as human hair and nails.

48. The lemur is a primate found only on the island of Madagascar.

49. The stripes of a zebra are believed to help camouflage them in tall grass and confuse predators, as well as cool their bodies through air circulation.

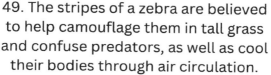

50. Lions are apex predators and are known for their hunting prowess, often taking down prey much larger than themselves.

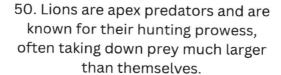

51. Lions have a lifespan of around 10-14 years in the wild, and up to 20 years in captivity.
Lion cubs are born with spots on their fur, which they lose as they grow older.

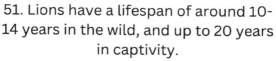

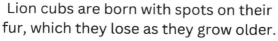

52. The roar of a lion can be heard from up to 5 miles (8 km) away.

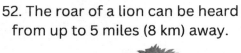

53. The scientific name for the lion is Panthera Leo.

54. While lions are often referred to as the "King of the jungle," they actually don't live in the jungle. Lions are primarily found in grasslands and savannas.

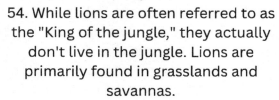

55. The mongoose is a small carnivorous mammal known for its ability to kill snakes.

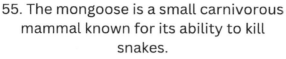

---

56. Tigers are the largest cat species in the world, with males weighing up to 660 pounds (300 kg) and females up to 370 pounds (170 kg).

---

57. Tigers are found primarily in Asia, with six subspecies still in existence today.

19

58. Tigers have a lifespan of around 10-15 years in the wild, and up to 20 years in captivity. The stripes on a tiger's coat are unique to each individual and can be used to identify them, much like a human fingerprint.

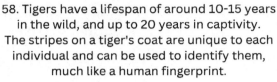
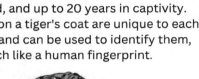

❖

59. Tigers are excellent swimmers and enjoy spending time in water to cool off. The roar of a tiger can be heard up to 2 miles (3 km) away.

❖

60. The scientific name for the tiger is Panthera Tigris.

20

61. Dogs are one of the oldest domesticated animals, with evidence of their existence dating back to over 30,000 years ago.

---

62. There are over 340 different breeds of dogs recognized by the World Canine Organization (WCO), each with unique physical and behavioral traits. The average lifespan of a dog ranges from 10-13 years, depending on the breed and size.

---

63. Certain breeds, such as the Golden Retriever and Labrador Retriever, are commonly used as service dogs for people with disabilities.

64. Dogs have an excellent hearing ability, and can hear sounds that are beyond the range of human ears. They also have a keen sense of time, and can sense when their owners are about to return home.

65. Puppies are born deaf and blind, and rely on their sense of smell and touch to navigate their environment.

66. Dogs were the first animals to be sent into space by the Soviet Union in 1957, named Laika.

  22

67. Horses are social animals and prefer to live in groups called herds or bands. They have a strong fight or flight response, which has allowed them to survive as prey animals for thousands of years.

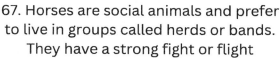

68. Horses have been used for transportation, work, and sports for thousands of years, and are still used for these purposes today. They have a keen sense of smell and hearing, which they use to detect danger and communicate with other horses.

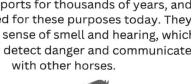

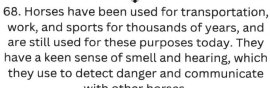

69. Horses are known for their speed and agility, with some breeds capable of reaching speeds of over 50 miles (80 kilometers) per hour.

70. The tongue of a giraffe is over 18 inches (45 cm) long and is blue-black in color. The tongue is so long that it can clean its own ears with it.

71. Elephants can communicate with each other through infrasonic sounds that are too low for human ears to hear.

72. The fingerprints of koalas are so similar to those of humans that they have been mistaken for each other at crime scenes.

73. Cows have best friends and can become stressed and anxious when separated from them.

---

74. Camels have a natural ability to conserve water, which allows them to survive in harsh desert conditions.

---

75. The tongue of a blue whale weighs as much as an adult elephant, which is around 6,000 to 7,000 pounds (2,700 to 3,200 kg).

25

76. The fennec fox, native to the Sahara Desert, has large ears that help it regulate its body temperature in the extreme heat.

77. In the winter, foxes may change the color of their fur to blend in with the snow, a process called "seasonal camouflage". They are known for their ability to store excess food for later, burying it in the ground or hiding it in crevices.

78. The honey badger is known for its fearless attitude and ability to take on animals many times its size, including lions and hyenas.

 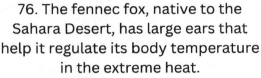

79. The gray wolf, also known as the timber wolf, is the largest member of the dog family, with males weighing up to 175 pounds (79 kilos).

---

80. Wolves have a highly developed sense of smell and can detect prey from over a mile away. They have powerful jaws and teeth, which they use to hunt and kill prey. They are able to exert over 1,500 pounds (680 kilos) of pressure per square inch with their bite.

---

81. Wolves mate for life and are very loyal to their partners and offspring. They are very vocal animals and use a variety of howls, barks, growls, and whines to communicate with each other.

82. Cats are one of the most popular pets in the world, with an estimated 95 million pet cats in the United States alone.

---

83. Cats are known for their agility and are able to jump up to six times their own body length in one leap.

---

84. Cats are crepuscular animals, meaning they are most active during the dawn and dusk hours. Cats are very clean animals and spend a large amount of time grooming themselves. They are also able to clean themselves using their rough tongues. Theyare able to retract their claws, which helps to keep them sharp and prevents them from wearing down when they are not being used.

85. Cheetahs are the only big cats that can purr, which they do when they are content or feeling calm. Unlike other big cats, cheetahs are not able to climb trees and are vulnerable to predators such as lions and hyenas.

86. Brown bears are one of the largest land mammals in the world, with males weighing up to 1,400 pounds and standing over 9 feet tall on their hind legs. They have a powerful sense of smell and can detect food from over a mile away.

87. Hedgehogs have up to 5000 spines on their body for protection.

88. Gorillas are the largest primates in the world, with males weighing up to 400 pounds (181 kilos) and standing up to 6 feet tall.

89. There are two species of gorillas: the western gorilla and the eastern gorilla, which includes the mountain gorilla and the eastern lowland gorilla.

90. Gorillas communicate with each other using a variety of vocalizations and gestures, such as chest-beating and grunting.
They are highly susceptible to human diseases and can be infected by illnesses such as the common cold or influenza, which can be fatal to them.

30

91. Giant pandas are one of the most endangered species in the world, with only around 1,800 left in the wild.

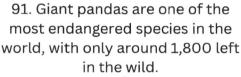

92. Pandas have a low reproductive rate and females only give birth to one or two cubs every two to three years.
Baby pandas are born pink and hairless, and are completely dependent on their mothers for the first few months of life.

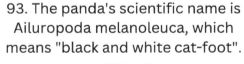

93. The panda's scientific name is Ailuropoda melanoleuca, which means "black and white cat-foot".

94. Dolphins are able to sleep with one eye open and one half of their brain awake, which allows them to remain alert to their surroundings and avoid predators.

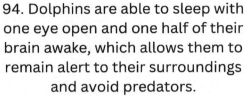

95. Llamas are capable of spitting as a means of defense or communication, and can accurately aim up to six feet away.

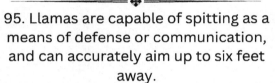

96. Goats have been domesticated for thousands of years and are believed to have been one of the first animals to be domesticated by humans.

97. Deer shed and regrow their antlers every year. Antlers can grow up to an inch per day and can weigh up to 40 pounds (18 kg).

---

98. Sheep are able to recognize up to 50 individual members of their flock, even after a long period of separation. They are not able to move their eyes independently, so they have to turn their heads to see in different directions.

---

99. White lions are a rare color mutation of the African lion and are not a separate species.

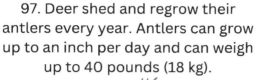
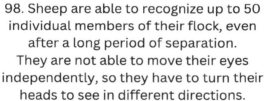

100. Humans are classified as mammals because they have hair, produce milk to nourish their young, and are warm-blooded. Humans have a lifespan that is longer than most mammals, with an average life expectancy of around 70 years.

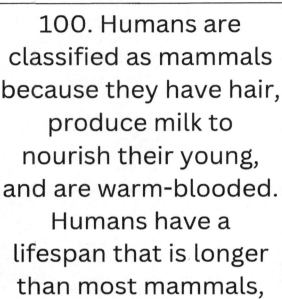

34

2- Birds

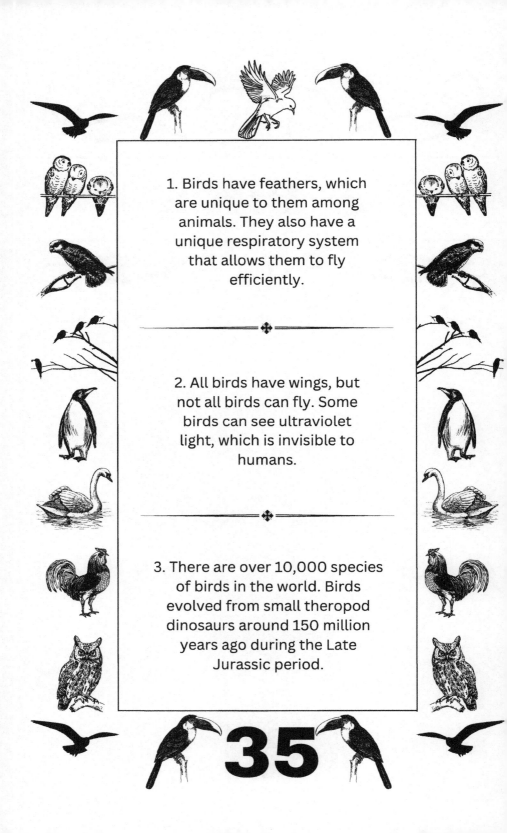

1. Birds have feathers, which are unique to them among animals. They also have a unique respiratory system that allows them to fly efficiently.

2. All birds have wings, but not all birds can fly. Some birds can see ultraviolet light, which is invisible to humans.

3. There are over 10,000 species of birds in the world. Birds evolved from small theropod dinosaurs around 150 million years ago during the Late Jurassic period.

4. The ostrich is the largest bird in the world and can weigh up to 350 pounds (159 kilos).

5. The bee hummingbird is the smallest bird in the world and weighs less than a penny.

6. Penguins are the only birds that can swim but not fly.

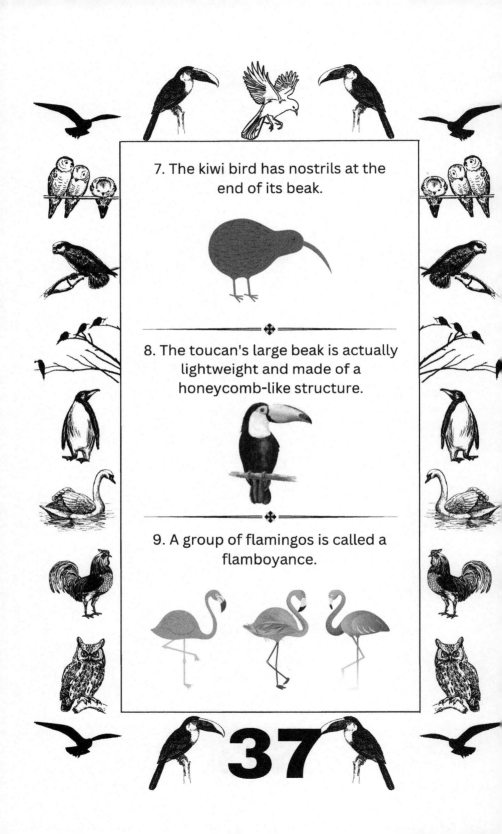

7. The kiwi bird has nostrils at the end of its beak.

8. The toucan's large beak is actually lightweight and made of a honeycomb-like structure.

9. A group of flamingos is called a flamboyance.

10. Some birds can mimic human speech, like parrots and mynas.

11. The peregrine falcon is the fastest bird and can dive at speeds over 200 mph (322 kph).

12. The hoatzin is the only bird in the world that has a digestive system similar to a cow's.

38

13. The male emperor penguin incubates the egg while the female goes hunting for food.

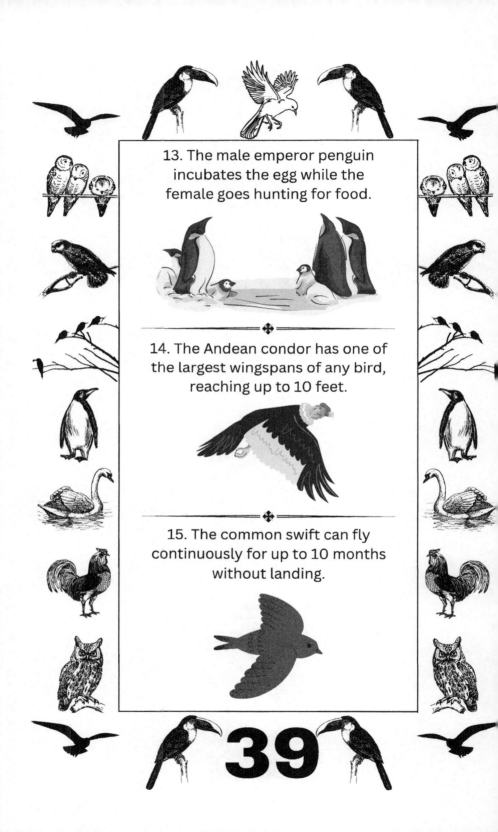

14. The Andean condor has one of the largest wingspans of any bird, reaching up to 10 feet.

15. The common swift can fly continuously for up to 10 months without landing.

16. Some birds, like the Arctic tern, are able to migrate incredible distances, with some individuals traveling over 44,000 miles (70,811 kilometers) in a single year.

17. The chicken is the most common bird in the world.

18. The African grey parrot has the intelligence of a 5-year-old human child.

19. Some birds, like the cuckoo, lay their eggs in other birds' nests and allow them to raise its young..

20. The woodpecker's tongue is so long that it wraps around its skull.

21. Owls are the only birds that can rotate their heads 270 degrees.

41

22. The flamingo's pink color comes from the carotenoid pigments in the algae and crustaceans they eat.

23. The albatross can sleep while flying, with one hemisphere of its brain at a time.

24. The bald eagle's nest, called an eyrie, can weigh up to a ton.

42

25. The turkey vulture has a sense of smell and can locate decaying animals from over a mile away.

26. The common loon's cry inspired the sound of the loon in the movie "Dumbo".

27. The Australian lyrebird can mimic any sound it hears, including chainsaws and car alarms.

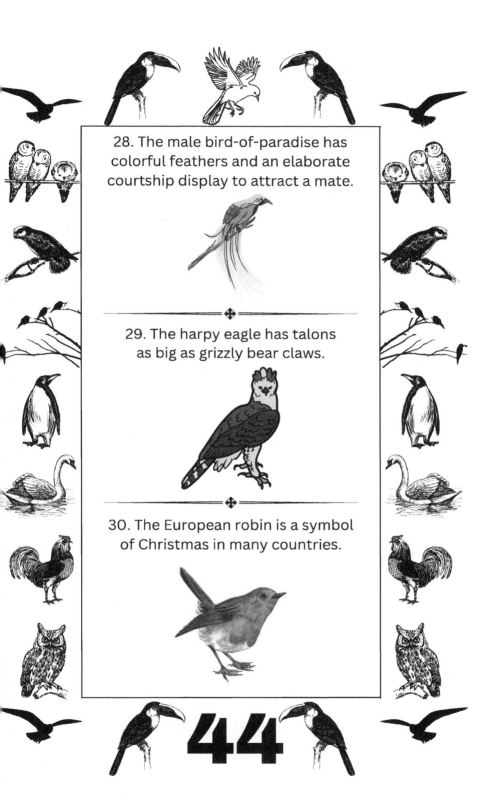

28. The male bird-of-paradise has colorful feathers and an elaborate courtship display to attract a mate.

29. The harpy eagle has talons as big as grizzly bear claws.

30. The European robin is a symbol of Christmas in many countries.

31. The hummingbird's heart beats up to 1,260 times per minute.

32. The rhea is the largest bird in South America and can run up to 40 mph (64 kph).

33. The male peacock displays its colorful feathers to attract a mate.

45

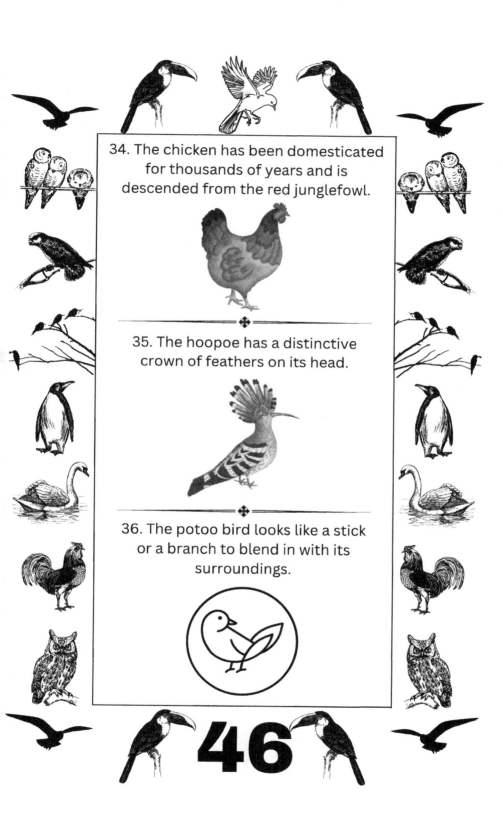

34. The chicken has been domesticated for thousands of years and is descended from the red junglefowl.

35. The hoopoe has a distinctive crown of feathers on its head.

36. The potoo bird looks like a stick or a branch to blend in with its surroundings.

46

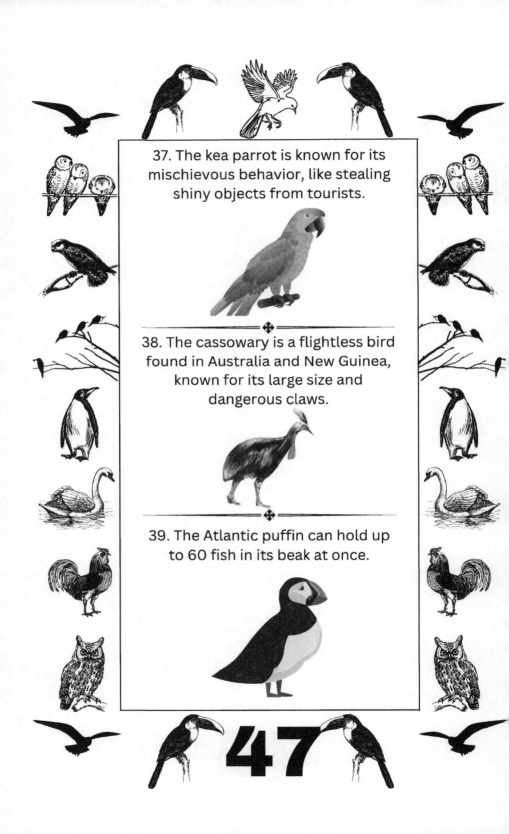

37. The kea parrot is known for its mischievous behavior, like stealing shiny objects from tourists.

38. The cassowary is a flightless bird found in Australia and New Guinea, known for its large size and dangerous claws.

39. The Atlantic puffin can hold up to 60 fish in its beak at once.

40. The black-capped chickadee can remember the locations of up to 1,000 individual seeds it has hidden.

41. The laughing kookaburra is a bird found in Australia known for its distinctive call, which sounds like human laughter.

42. The male superb lyrebird builds a complex and elaborate display mound to attract a mate.

48

43. The oilbird, found in South America, is the only bird in the world that uses echolocation to navigate in complete darkness.

44. The male sage grouse performs an elaborate dance during mating season, puffing up its chest and making a deep, resonant sound.

45. The European starling, introduced to North America in the late 1800s, is now one of the most common and widespread birds on the continent.

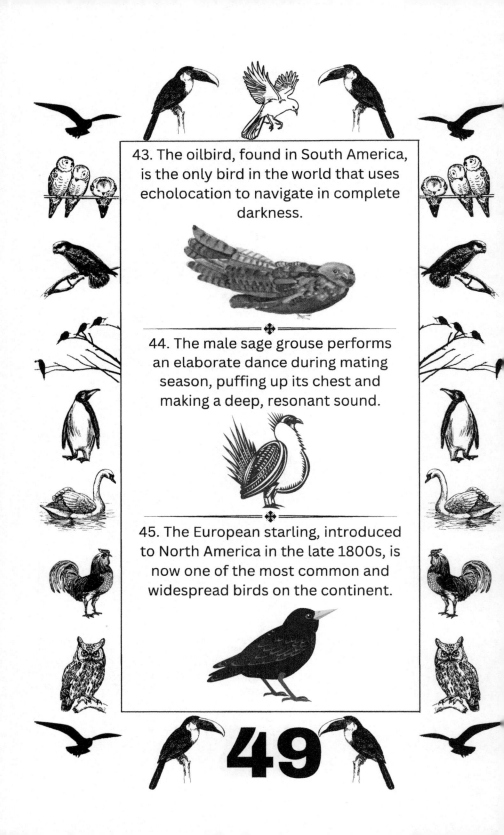

49

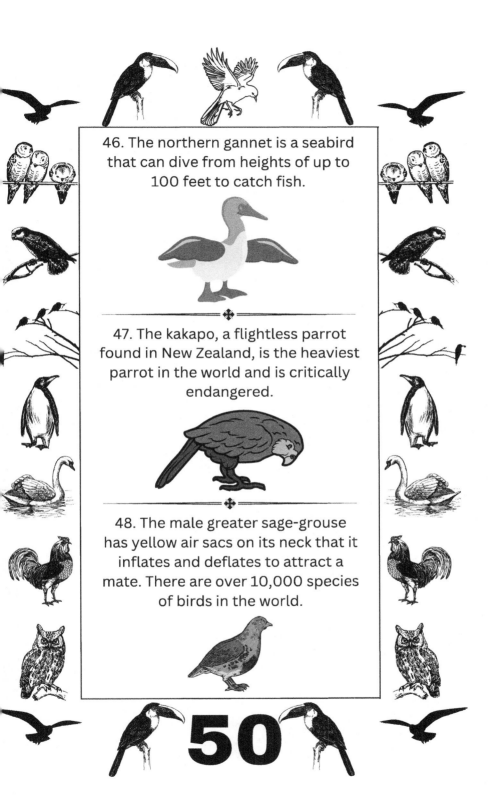

46. The northern gannet is a seabird that can dive from heights of up to 100 feet to catch fish.

47. The kakapo, a flightless parrot found in New Zealand, is the heaviest parrot in the world and is critically endangered.

48. The male greater sage-grouse has yellow air sacs on its neck that it inflates and deflates to attract a mate. There are over 10,000 species of birds in the world.

50

49. The barn owl has asymmetrical ears that allow it to locate prey in complete darkness.

---

50. The kestrel, a type of falcon, can hover in mid-air while hunting for prey.

---

51. The male blue-footed booby displays its bright blue feet during courtship.

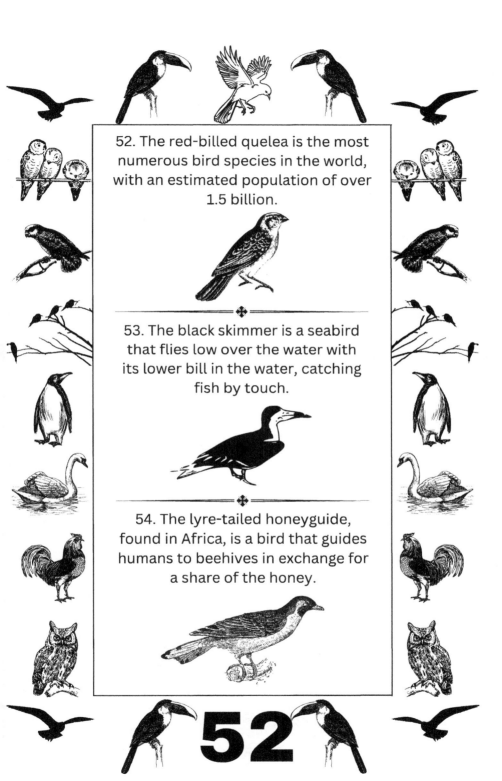

52. The red-billed quelea is the most numerous bird species in the world, with an estimated population of over 1.5 billion.

53. The black skimmer is a seabird that flies low over the water with its lower bill in the water, catching fish by touch.

54. The lyre-tailed honeyguide, found in Africa, is a bird that guides humans to beehives in exchange for a share of the honey.

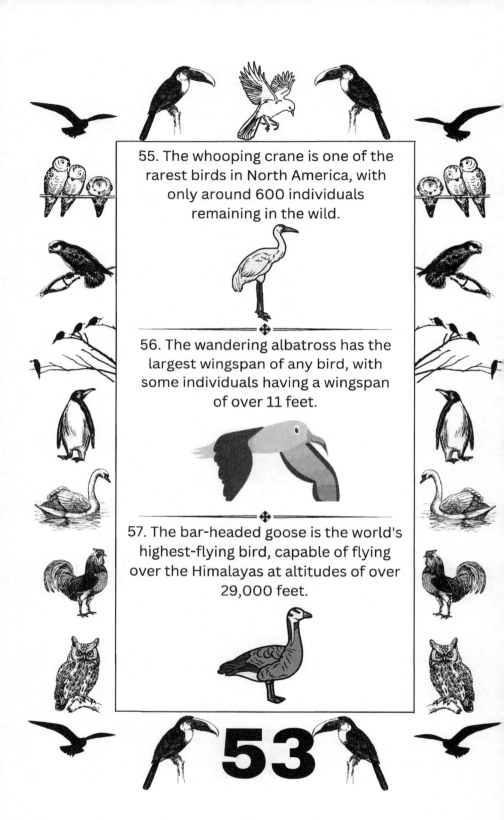

55. The whooping crane is one of the rarest birds in North America, with only around 600 individuals remaining in the wild.

56. The wandering albatross has the largest wingspan of any bird, with some individuals having a wingspan of over 11 feet.

57. The bar-headed goose is the world's highest-flying bird, capable of flying over the Himalayas at altitudes of over 29,000 feet.

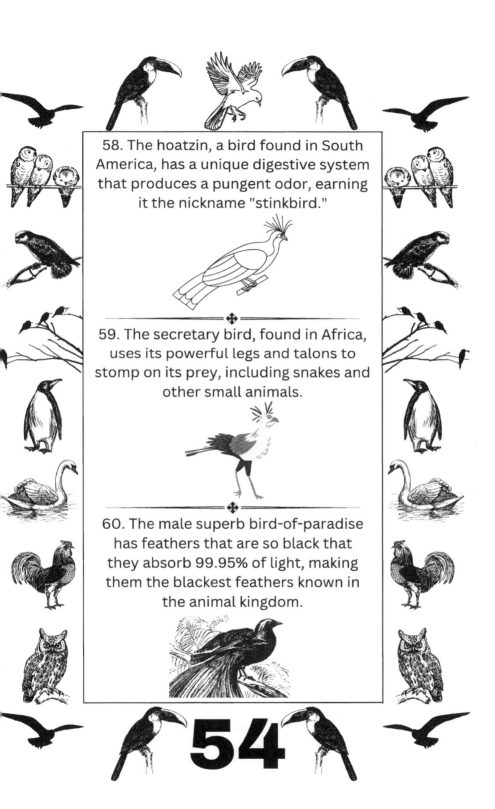

58. The hoatzin, a bird found in South America, has a unique digestive system that produces a pungent odor, earning it the nickname "stinkbird."

❖

59. The secretary bird, found in Africa, uses its powerful legs and talons to stomp on its prey, including snakes and other small animals.

❖

60. The male superb bird-of-paradise has feathers that are so black that they absorb 99.95% of light, making them the blackest feathers known in the animal kingdom.

61. The helmeted hornbill, found in Southeast Asia, has a solid ivory casque on its bill that is highly valued in illegal wildlife trade.

62. The greater roadrunner, found in the southwestern United States, is capable of running at speeds of up to 20 miles (32 kilometers) per hour.

63. The Andean condor is one of the heaviest flying birds in the world, with some individuals weighing over 30 pounds (13.6 kilos).

64. The northern cardinal, found in North America, has the ability to sing two different songs at the same time, a talent known as "duetting."

65. Eagles are capable of flying at high speeds, with some species capable of reaching speeds of over 100 miles (161 kilometers) per hour during a dive.

66. Golden eagles, found throughout much of the northern hemisphere, are known for their incredible hunting skills and have been trained for falconry for thousands of years.

67. The bald eagle was once on the brink of extinction due to habitat loss and hunting, but has made a remarkable recovery thanks to conservation efforts and the banning of the pesticide DDT.

68. Penguins have a unique method of moving on land, known as "tobogganing," in which they slide along the ice on their bellies using their flippers and feet to propel themselves forward.

69. Penguins can hold their breath for several minutes while underwater, and are capable of diving to depths of over 500 feet.

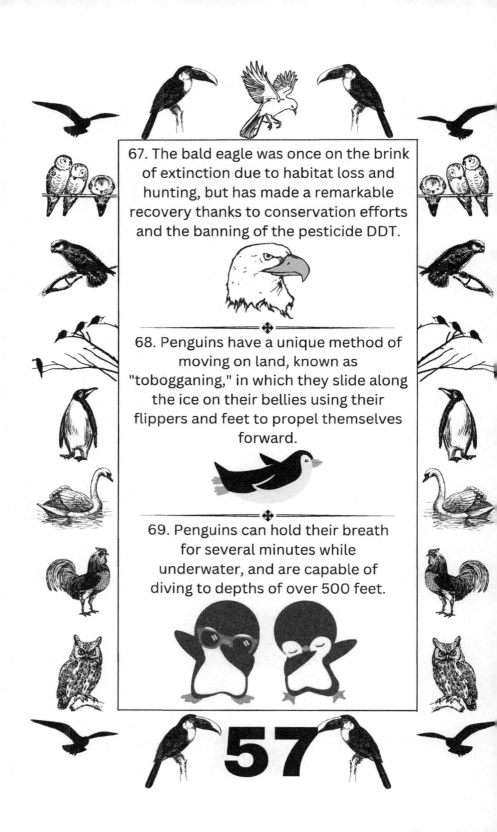

70. Penguins are often associated with the Christmas holiday due to their appearance in popular culture, such as in the movie "Happy Feet" and the John Lewis Christmas advert.

71. Falcons have sharp talons and beaks that they use to catch and kill their prey, which can include small mammals, birds, and insects.

72. Falcons are often used in falconry, a traditional hunting method that involves training falcons to hunt prey for humans.

73. Hawks have excellent eyesight, which they use to spot prey from high in the sky, and can see up to eight times better than humans.

74. Many species of hawks are migratory and travel long distances each year in search of food and suitable breeding grounds.

75. Hawks build nests, or eyries, in high places such as trees or cliffs, and often return to the same nest year after year.

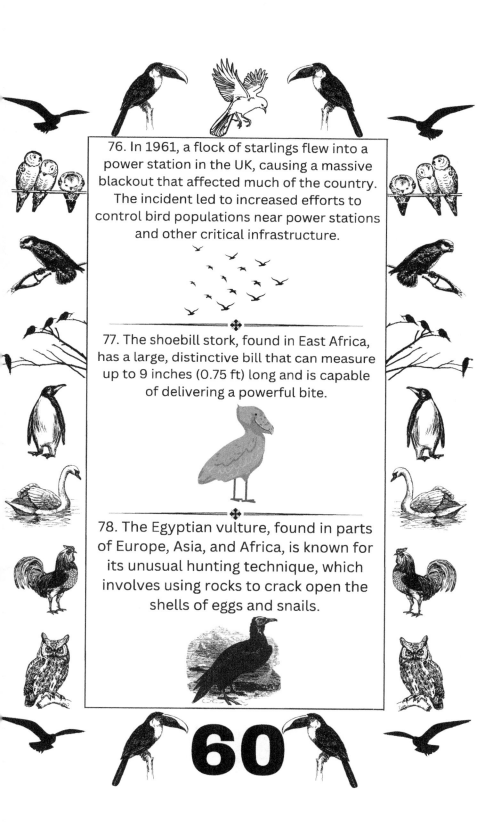

76. In 1961, a flock of starlings flew into a power station in the UK, causing a massive blackout that affected much of the country. The incident led to increased efforts to control bird populations near power stations and other critical infrastructure.

77. The shoebill stork, found in East Africa, has a large, distinctive bill that can measure up to 9 inches (0.75 ft) long and is capable of delivering a powerful bite.

78. The Egyptian vulture, found in parts of Europe, Asia, and Africa, is known for its unusual hunting technique, which involves using rocks to crack open the shells of eggs and snails.

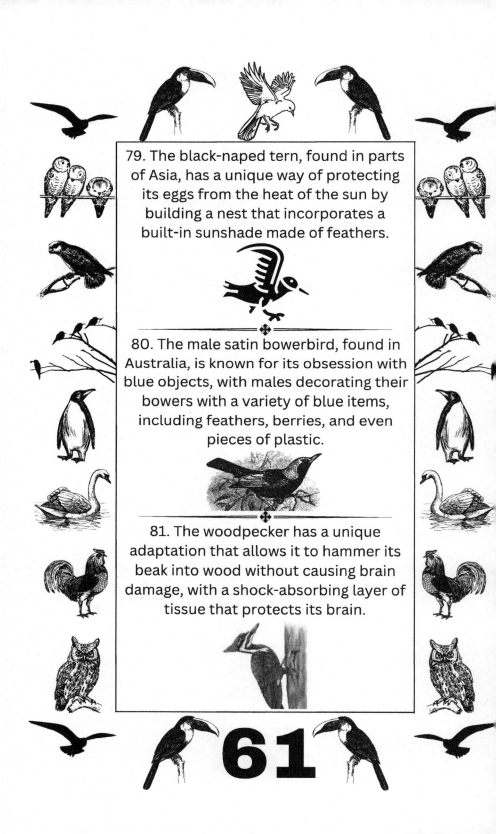

79. The black-naped tern, found in parts of Asia, has a unique way of protecting its eggs from the heat of the sun by building a nest that incorporates a built-in sunshade made of feathers.

80. The male satin bowerbird, found in Australia, is known for its obsession with blue objects, with males decorating their bowers with a variety of blue items, including feathers, berries, and even pieces of plastic.

81. The woodpecker has a unique adaptation that allows it to hammer its beak into wood without causing brain damage, with a shock-absorbing layer of tissue that protects its brain.

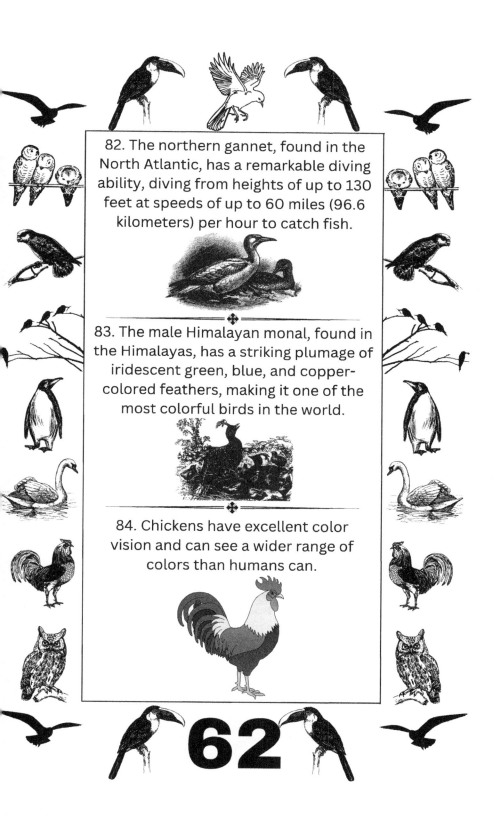

82. The northern gannet, found in the North Atlantic, has a remarkable diving ability, diving from heights of up to 130 feet at speeds of up to 60 miles (96.6 kilometers) per hour to catch fish.

83. The male Himalayan monal, found in the Himalayas, has a striking plumage of iridescent green, blue, and copper-colored feathers, making it one of the most colorful birds in the world.

84. Chickens have excellent color vision and can see a wider range of colors than humans can.

85. The world's largest chicken egg weighed nearly 12 ounces (340 grams) and had a circumference of over 7 inches (0.58 ft).

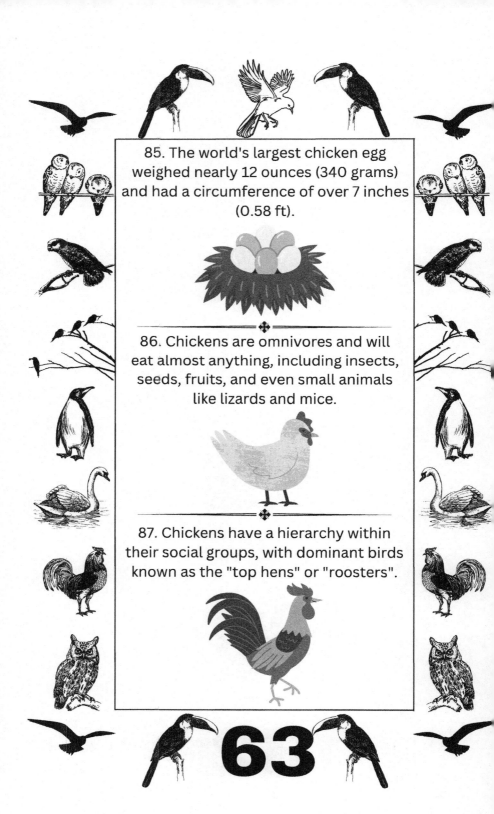

86. Chickens are omnivores and will eat almost anything, including insects, seeds, fruits, and even small animals like lizards and mice.

87. Chickens have a hierarchy within their social groups, with dominant birds known as the "top hens" or "roosters".

88. Ducks are water birds and are adapted for swimming and diving, with webbed feet and waterproof feathers.

89. Ducks have a unique digestive system that allows them to extract nutrients from their food very efficiently, which is important for their survival in the wild.

90. Ducks have an oil gland at the base of their tail that produces oil, which they use to coat their feathers and make them waterproof.

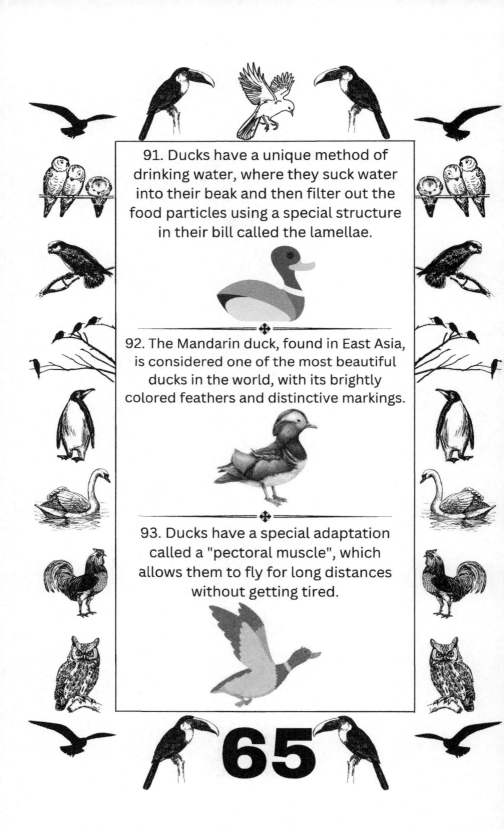

91. Ducks have a unique method of drinking water, where they suck water into their beak and then filter out the food particles using a special structure in their bill called the lamellae.

92. The Mandarin duck, found in East Asia, is considered one of the most beautiful ducks in the world, with its brightly colored feathers and distinctive markings.

93. Ducks have a special adaptation called a "pectoral muscle", which allows them to fly for long distances without getting tired.

65

94. Birds have a unique respiratory system, with a set of air sacs that allow them to take in oxygen more efficiently than mammals.

95. The oldest known bird fossil is that of the Archaeopteryx, which lived around 150 million years ago and is considered to be the missing link between dinosaurs and birds.

96. Slothful sheathbill is found in the sub-Antarctic regions. It is known for its lack of motivation and its tendency to beg for food rather than hunt or scavenge for it.

97. Swans are monogamous, meaning that they mate for life. Although they are typically thought of as being white, there are actually some species, such as the black swan, that have black feathers.

98. Swan Lake is a famous ballet composed by Pyotr Ilyich Tchaikovsky, and it tells the story of a princess named Odette who is transformed into a swan by an evil sorcerer.

99. During courtship, swans will perform an elaborate "dance" where they swim in synchronized circles around each other.

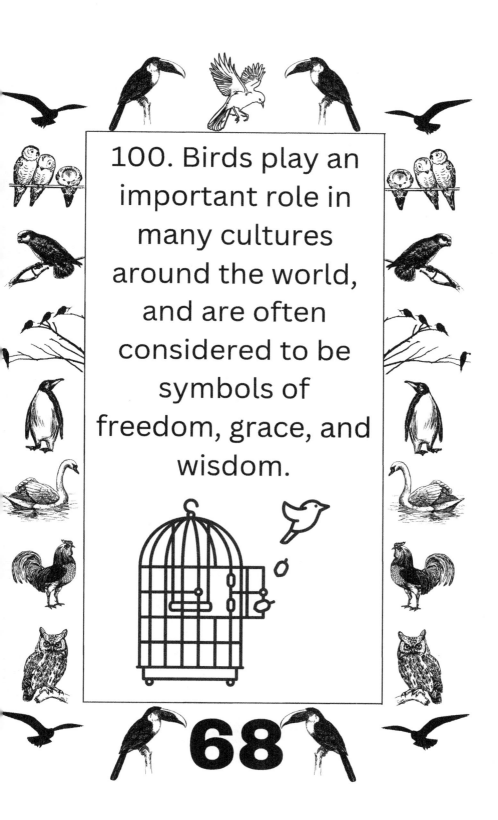

100. Birds play an important role in many cultures around the world, and are often considered to be symbols of freedom, grace, and wisdom.

68

3- Fish

1. Fish are cold-blooded animals that live in water and breathe through gills. They can be found in almost every aquatic environment, including freshwater, saltwater, and even underground caves.

❖

2. Fish have a lateral line system that runs down their sides, which helps them detect movement and vibrations in the water.

 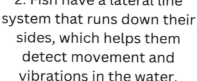 

❖

3. There are over 30,000 species of fish, making them the most diverse group of vertebrates on Earth. Fish are one of the oldest groups of animals on the planet and have been around for a very long time, with the earliest known fish-like creatures dating back over 500 million years.

 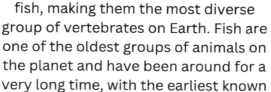 

 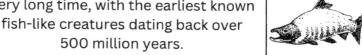

 **69**

4. The largest fish in the world is the whale shark (Rhincodon typus), which can grow up to 12.65 meters (41.5 feet) long and weigh up to 21.5 tonnes (21,319 kg).

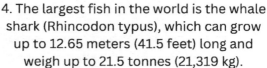

5. The smallest fish in the world is the Paedocypris fish, which is only 7.9mm (0.3 inches) long.

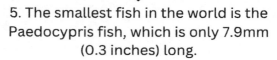

6. The longest living fish is the Greenland shark (Somniosus microcephalus), which is also one of the slowest-growing fish in the world. These sharks have been known to live for more than 400 years, making them the longest-lived vertebrates on the planet.

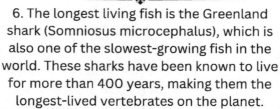

70

7. Clownfish, such as the famous Nemo, are born male but can change their gender to female later in life.

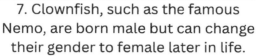

❖

8. Electric eels are not actually eels, but a type of knifefish. They are capable of producing electric shocks of up to 600 volts, which they use to navigate and stun prey.

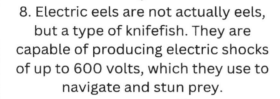

❖

9. The anglerfish has a long, protruding spine on its head that contains a bioluminescent lure to attract prey.

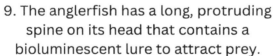

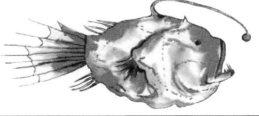

10. The mudskipper fish is capable of breathing air and can even crawl on land, using its pectoral fins to move around.

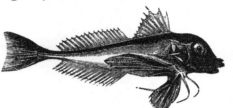

11. The sailfish is considered the fastest fish in the world, capable of swimming at speeds of up to 68 miles per hour (110 km/h).

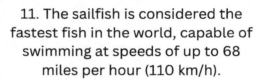

12. The Archerfish has a unique hunting strategy in which it shoots jets of water at insects above the water's surface, knocking them into the water where they can be eaten.

13. The Siamese fighting fish, also known as the Betta fish, is a popular aquarium fish known for its bright colors and aggressive behavior towards other male fish of the same species.

✛

14. The pacu fish, a close relative of the piranha, has human-like teeth that are used to crush hard nuts and seeds.

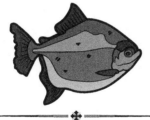

✛

15. The seahorse is the only fish species in which the male carries and gives birth to the offspring.

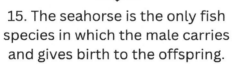

16. The blobfish, a deep-sea fish found off the coast of Australia, is known for its unusual appearance, which has earned it the title of "the world's ugliest fish".

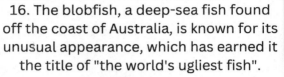

17. The lionfish is a venomous fish that has been introduced to non-native areas and has become an invasive species, causing harm to local ecosystems.

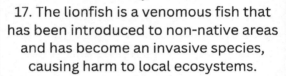

18. The coelacanth is a primitive fish that was once thought to be extinct but was rediscovered in 1938 off the coast of South Africa. It is known for its unique features, including its large size and its fleshy, lobed fins.

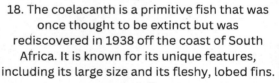

19. The goblin shark is a deep-sea shark with a distinctive long, protruding snout that it uses to sense prey.

❖

20. The deep-sea hatchetfish is a small, bioluminescent fish that uses its light-producing organs to attract prey and communicate with other members of its species.

❖

21. The pufferfish is a popular delicacy in Japan but can be deadly if not prepared correctly, as some parts of the fish contain a potent neurotoxin.

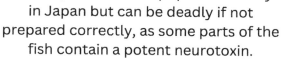

22. The manta ray is a large, gentle fish that feeds on plankton and is known for its graceful swimming style.

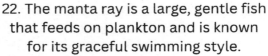

23. The triggerfish gets its name from its ability to lock its dorsal fin in place, making it difficult for predators to attack it.

❖

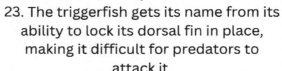

24. The tilapia is a popular food fish that is farmed in many parts of the world. It is known for its mild taste and versatility in cooking.

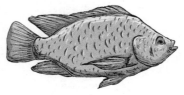

25. The flying fish is a species of fish that can leap out of the water and glide through the air for distances of up to 200 meters (656 feet) to escape from predators.

26. The electric catfish is a freshwater fish that is capable of producing electric shocks of up to 350 volts, which it uses to navigate and communicate with other members of its species.

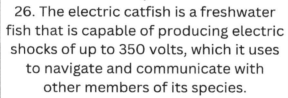

27. The swordfish is a large, predatory fish that uses its long bill to slash and stun its prey.

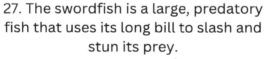

28. The piranha is a carnivorous fish that is known for its sharp teeth and aggressive behavior. However, not all piranhas are dangerous to humans, and some species are actually herbivorous.

---

29. The seadragon is a type of fish that is closely related to the seahorse. It is known for its intricate, leaf-like appendages that help it to blend in with its surroundings.

---

30. The stonefish is one of the most venomous fish in the world and is capable of causing severe pain and even death in humans.

31. The salmon is a migratory fish that spends most of its life in the ocean but returns to freshwater rivers and streams to spawn.

32. The tuna is a popular food fish that is known for its large size and fast swimming speed. Some species of tuna, such as the bluefin tuna, are endangered due to overfishing.

33. The jellyfish is a type of free-swimming marine animal that is known for its translucent, bell-shaped body and stinging tentacles. Jellyfish are not really fish. A fish's anatomy is centered around its backbone. The jellyfish is an invertebrate.

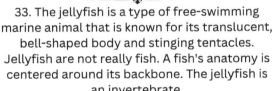

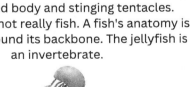

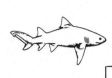

34. The halibut is a large, flatfish that is commonly caught for food. It is known for its mild, flaky white flesh and is often served baked or grilled.

---❖---

35. The sturgeon is a large, ancient fish that is known for its prized caviar. Some species of sturgeon can live up to 100 years.

---❖---

36. The gourami is a popular aquarium fish that is known for its bright colors and unique behaviors, such as building bubble nests for its eggs.

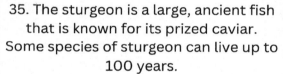

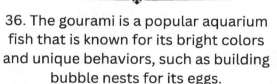

37. The barracuda is a predatory fish that is found in warm, tropical waters. It is known for its sharp teeth and fast swimming speed.

38. The marlin is a large, predatory fish that is popular among sport fishermen. It is known for its long, spear-like bill and its fast swimming speed.

39. The herring is a small, oily fish that is commonly used for bait and as a food source for humans. It is known for its high nutritional value and is rich in omega-3 fatty acids.

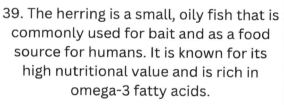

40. The axolotl is a type of salamander that is native to Mexico. It is capable of regenerating lost limbs and is used in scientific research to study regeneration.

---

41. The gobies are a large family of small, colorful fish that are found in freshwater and saltwater environments around the world.

---

42. The mahi-mahi is a popular game fish that is found in tropical waters around the world. It is known for its bright colors and fast swimming speed.

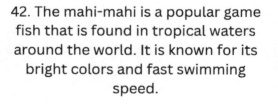

43. The sevengill shark is a large, deep-water shark that is found in oceans around the world.

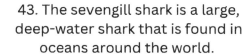

❖

44. The mud eel is a type of fish that is found in freshwater and is capable of living out of water for extended periods of time. It is also known as the "walking fish" because it can move across land using its pectoral fins.

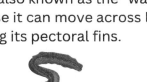

❖

45. The cuttlefish is a type of cephalopod that is known for its ability to change color and texture to blend in with its surroundings. It is also used as a popular aquarium species.

46. The catfish is a type of bottom-dwelling fish that is found in freshwater environments around the world. It is named for its whisker-like barbels, which are used to detect food.

47. The guppy is a small, colorful freshwater fish that is popular in the aquarium trade. It is known for its hardiness and ease of care.

48. The suckerfish is a type of fish that is named for its suction cup-like mouth, which it uses to attach itself to other fish or surfaces.

49. The lanternfish is a deep-sea fish that is known for its ability to produce light through bioluminescence. It is an important food source for larger marine animals.

50. The weedy sea dragon is a type of seahorse that is found in the waters off southern Australia. It is known for its unique, weed-like appearance and its ability to blend in with its surroundings.

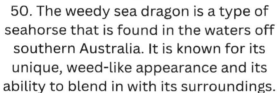

51. The koi is a type of ornamental carp that is popular in Japanese culture. It is known for its vibrant colors and its association with luck and prosperity.

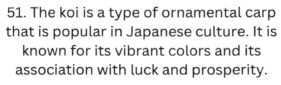

52. The wrasse is a type of fish that is found in tropical and subtropical waters around the world. It is known for its unique, elongated shape and its ability to change colors.

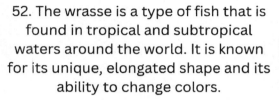

---

53. The stone loach is a small, freshwater fish that is found in Europe and Asia. It is known for its ability to climb up steep, slippery surfaces using its specialized pelvic fins.

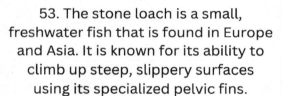

---

54. The archerfish is a type of fish that is found in the waters of Southeast Asia and Australia. It is known for its ability to shoot down insects and other prey with a stream of water.

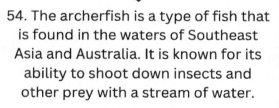

55. The pufferfish is a type of fish that is found in tropical and subtropical waters around the world. It is known for its ability to inflate itself into a ball-like shape as a defense mechanism.

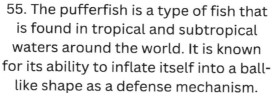

56. The triggerfish is a tropical marine fish that is known for its unique shape and vibrant colors. It is named for the trigger-like mechanism on its dorsal fin.

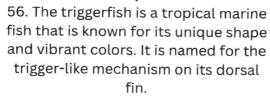

57. The lionfish It is known for its striking appearance and its ability to rapidly expand its spiny fins as a defense mechanism.

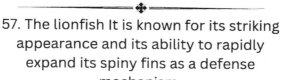
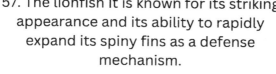

58. The clownfish is known for its symbiotic relationship with sea anemones, which provide protection for the fish.

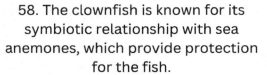

---

59. The moray eel is a type of eel that is found in tropical and subtropical waters around the world. It is known for its long, serpentine body and its sharp teeth.

---

60. The stargazer is a type of fish that is found in shallow waters around the world. It is named for its upward-facing eyes, which are used to ambush prey from below.

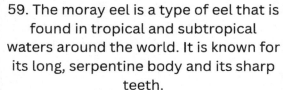

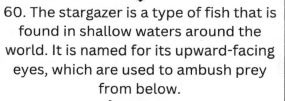

61. The great white shark is perhaps the most famous shark, known for its large size and fearsome reputation. It can grow up to 20 feet in length and weigh over 4,000 pounds (1,814 kilos).

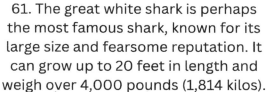

✦

62. The whale shark (the largest fish), despite its size, it is a gentle giant that feeds primarily on plankton.

✦

63. The hammerhead shark is known for its distinctive head shape, which allows it to see more efficiently and catch prey more effectively.

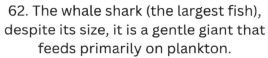

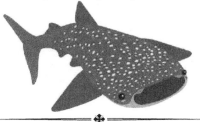

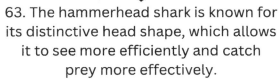

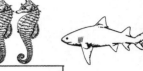

64. The tiger shark is one of the largest predatory sharks in the world and is known for its voracious appetite. It has been known to eat everything from sea turtles to license plates.

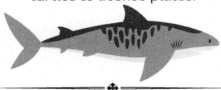

❖

65. The bull shark is a dangerous species of shark that is known for its aggressive behavior and ability to swim in freshwater as well as saltwater.

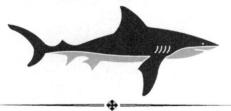

❖

66. The nurse shark is a docile species of shark that is found primarily in shallow waters. It is known for its slow-moving, sedentary lifestyle.

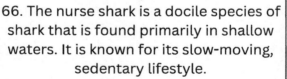

67. The blue shark is a long, slender shark that is found in open ocean environments. It is known for its distinctive blue coloration and its ability to swim long distances.

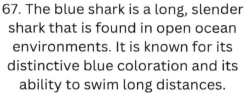

68. The lemon shark is a relatively small species of shark that is found in shallow, tropical waters. It is named for its yellowish-brown coloration.

69. The goblin shark is rarely seen by humans.

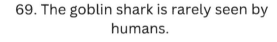

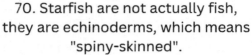

70. Starfish are not actually fish, they are echinoderms, which means "spiny-skinned".
They are also known as sea stars, and there are over 2,000 species of them in the world.

---

71. Goldfish are a species of freshwater fish that belong to the carp family.
They are known for their ability to live in a variety of different environments, including aquariums, ponds, and even bowls.

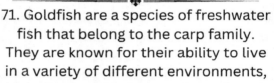
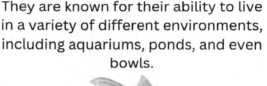

---

72. Goldfish have a good memory and are capable of learning and recognizing their owners.
They are a popular pet around the world and are often given as prizes at fairs and carnivals. However, it's important to remember that goldfish require proper care and attention to thrive.

73. Carp is a common name for several species of freshwater fish belonging to the family Cyprinidae.
Carps are native to Asia and Europe, but have been introduced to many other parts of the world.

74. The ocean sunfish is the heaviest bony fish in the world and can weigh up to 2,200 pounds.

75. The Atlantic salmon is a species of fish that is famous for its ability to navigate long distances to spawn in the same river where it was born.

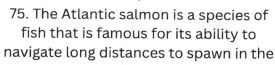

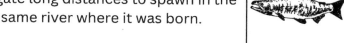

76. The red-bellied piranha is a carnivorous species of fish that is known for its sharp teeth and reputation as a fierce predator.

77. The blacktip reef shark is a common species of shark found in shallow waters around coral reefs, and is known for its distinctive black-tipped fins.

78. The tarpon is a large, silver-colored fish that is prized by sport fishermen for its acrobatic jumps and impressive strength.

79. The catfish is known for its whisker-like barbels and bottom-dwelling behavior.

---

80. The sevengill shark is named for its seven gill slits, which are unusual for sharks (most sharks have five).

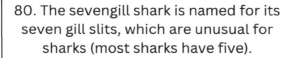

---

81. The arapaima is a massive freshwater fish found in the Amazon River basin, and can grow up to 10 feet long and weigh over 400 pounds.

82. The Mantis Shrimp has the most complex eyesight of any known animal, capable of detecting polarized light, ultraviolet light, and even having 16 color-receptive cones.

83. The hagfish has the unique ability to produce large amounts of slime when threatened, which can clog the gills of predators and suffocate them.

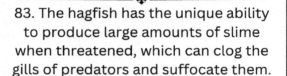

84. Hagfish have no jaws, but instead have a ring of tentacles around their mouth that they use to rasp flesh off their prey.
They are scavengers and are known to feed on dead or dying animals that sink to the ocean floor.

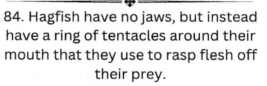

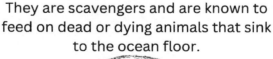

96

85. The paddlefish has a unique snout that is used to detect and capture prey in murky waters, and can grow up to 7 feet long.

86. Paddlefish are filter feeders, using their gill rakers to strain tiny zooplankton and small invertebrates from the water. They are a long-lived species, with some individuals living up to 30 years in the wild.

87. The tasselled wobbegong is a species of carpet shark that has a unique camouflage pattern on its skin that allows it to blend in with the seafloor and ambush prey.

88. Bluefin tuna are some of the largest and fastest fish in the ocean. They are highly valued for their meat and can fetch high prices at markets.

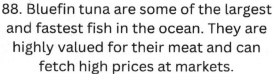

❖

89. The zebrafish is a small freshwater fish native to South Asia. It has become a popular model organism in genetic and developmental research due to its fast reproductive rate, transparency of its embryos, and ability to regenerate damaged tissue.

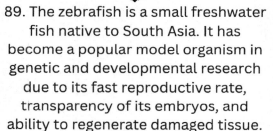

❖

90. Octopuses are not actually fish. They belong to a different class of animals called cephalopods, which also includes squids, cuttlefish, and nautiluses. Unlike fish, cephalopods do not have a backbone and instead have a soft body with a ring of tentacles or arms around their head.

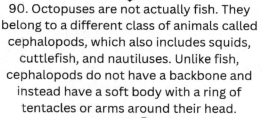

91. The rainbow trout is a popular freshwater fish found in streams and rivers throughout North America. It is known for its bright colors and its popularity as a game fish, prized by anglers for its fighting ability and tasty flesh.

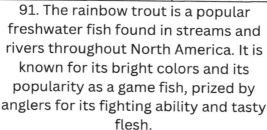

92. The salmon shark is a large shark species found in the North Pacific Ocean. It is known for its unique ability to regulate its body temperature, allowing it to swim in cold waters where other shark species cannot survive.

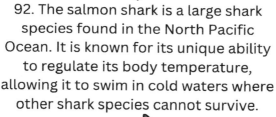

93. The opah, also known as the moonfish, is a deep-sea fish found in the Atlantic, Indian, and Pacific Oceans. It is unique in that it is warm-blooded, able to maintain its body temperature higher than the surrounding water.

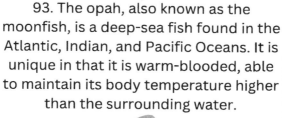

94. The Royal Blue Tang, also known as the regal tang, is a popular marine fish that is native to the Pacific Ocean. It is a small fish that typically grows up to 30 cm (12 inches) in length, with a bright blue body and yellow tail fin.

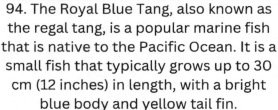

---

95. The Royal Blue Tang is a shoaling fish, meaning it likes to live in groups with other Royal Blue Tangs or other similar species. It is also known as the "Dory" fish, due to its resemblance to the character of Dory in the animated film "Finding Nemo".

---

96. The Royal Blue Tang is capable of changing its coloration depending on its mood, with brighter colors indicating a happy and healthy fish.

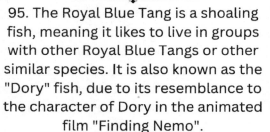

100

97. Guppies are small and brightly colored fish that are popular in aquariums. They are native to South America but have been introduced to many parts of the world due to their popularity as pets.

98. Grouper are large, slow-moving fish that are found in warm waters around the world. They are prized by fishermen for their meat, which is considered a delicacy in many countries.

99. Cods are cold-water fish that are found in the Atlantic and Pacific Oceans. They are a popular food fish and are used in many dishes around the world, including fish and chips.

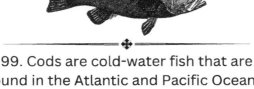

101

100. Many fish species are important for human consumption, providing an important source of protein and omega-3 fatty acids.

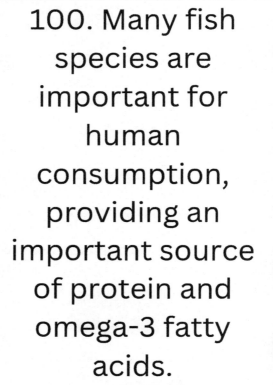

102

4- Reptiles

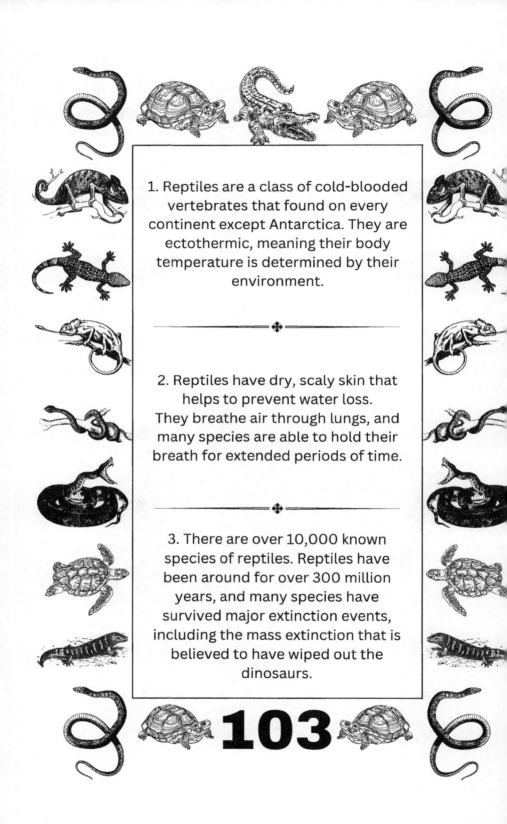

1. Reptiles are a class of cold-blooded vertebrates that found on every continent except Antarctica. They are ectothermic, meaning their body temperature is determined by their environment.

---

2. Reptiles have dry, scaly skin that helps to prevent water loss. They breathe air through lungs, and many species are able to hold their breath for extended periods of time.

---

3. There are over 10,000 known species of reptiles. Reptiles have been around for over 300 million years, and many species have survived major extinction events, including the mass extinction that is believed to have wiped out the dinosaurs.

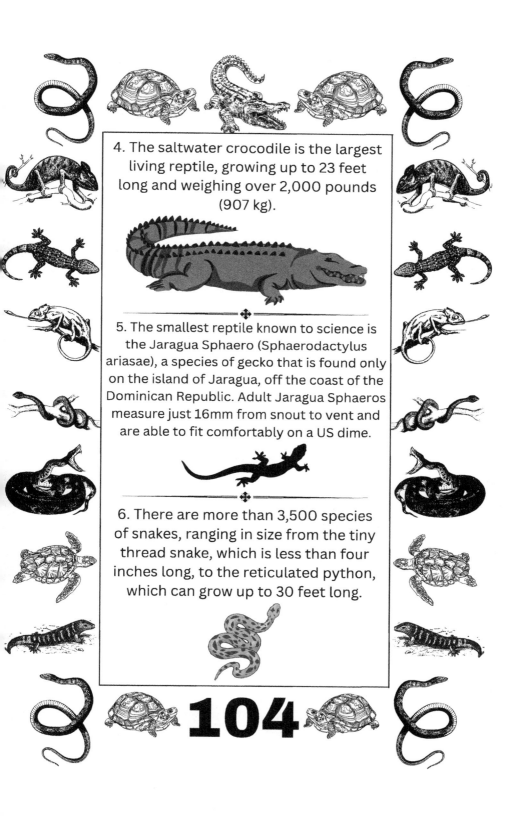

4. The saltwater crocodile is the largest living reptile, growing up to 23 feet long and weighing over 2,000 pounds (907 kg).

5. The smallest reptile known to science is the Jaragua Sphaero (Sphaerodactylus ariasae), a species of gecko that is found only on the island of Jaragua, off the coast of the Dominican Republic. Adult Jaragua Sphaeros measure just 16mm from snout to vent and are able to fit comfortably on a US dime.

6. There are more than 3,500 species of snakes, ranging in size from the tiny thread snake, which is less than four inches long, to the reticulated python, which can grow up to 30 feet long.

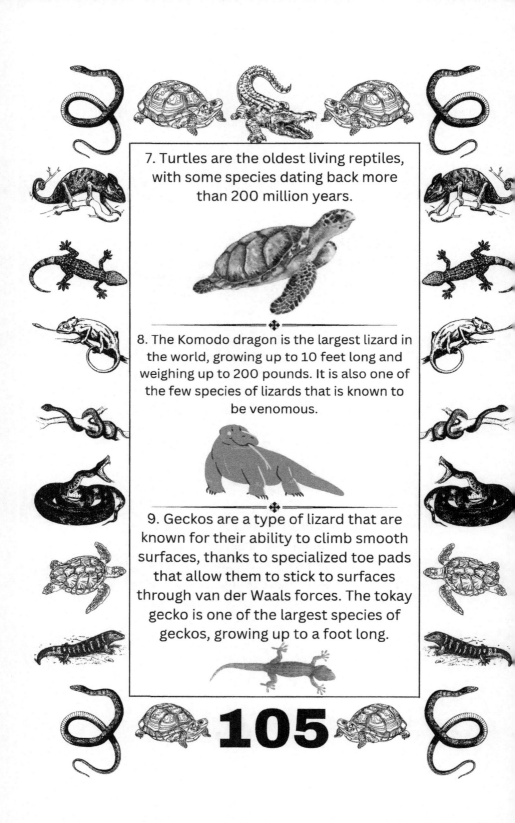

7. Turtles are the oldest living reptiles, with some species dating back more than 200 million years.

8. The Komodo dragon is the largest lizard in the world, growing up to 10 feet long and weighing up to 200 pounds. It is also one of the few species of lizards that is known to be venomous.

9. Geckos are a type of lizard that are known for their ability to climb smooth surfaces, thanks to specialized toe pads that allow them to stick to surfaces through van der Waals forces. The tokay gecko is one of the largest species of geckos, growing up to a foot long.

10. Chameleons are known for their ability to change color, which they use for communication and to regulate their body temperature. They also have long, sticky tongues that they use to catch prey.

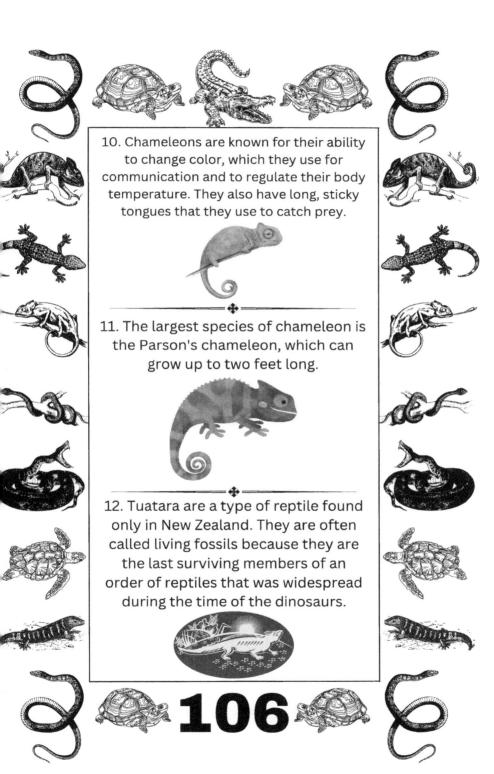

---

11. The largest species of chameleon is the Parson's chameleon, which can grow up to two feet long.

---

12. Tuatara are a type of reptile found only in New Zealand. They are often called living fossils because they are the last surviving members of an order of reptiles that was widespread during the time of the dinosaurs.

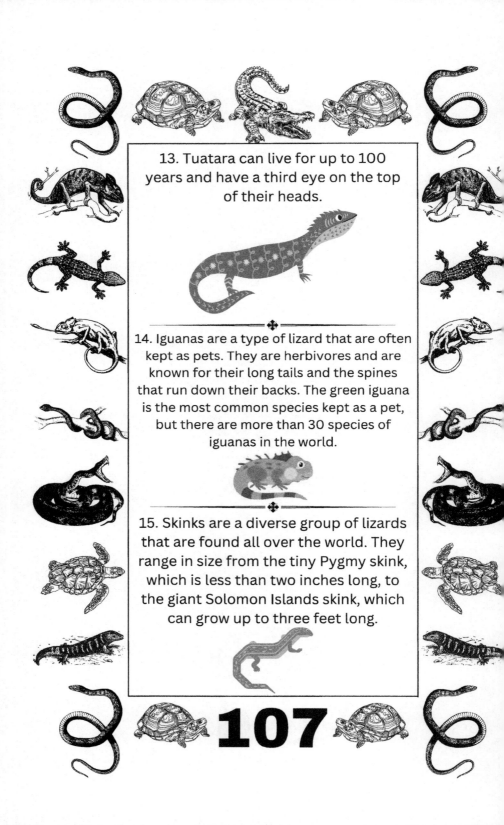

13. Tuatara can live for up to 100 years and have a third eye on the top of their heads.

14. Iguanas are a type of lizard that are often kept as pets. They are herbivores and are known for their long tails and the spines that run down their backs. The green iguana is the most common species kept as a pet, but there are more than 30 species of iguanas in the world.

15. Skinks are a diverse group of lizards that are found all over the world. They range in size from the tiny Pygmy skink, which is less than two inches long, to the giant Solomon Islands skink, which can grow up to three feet long.

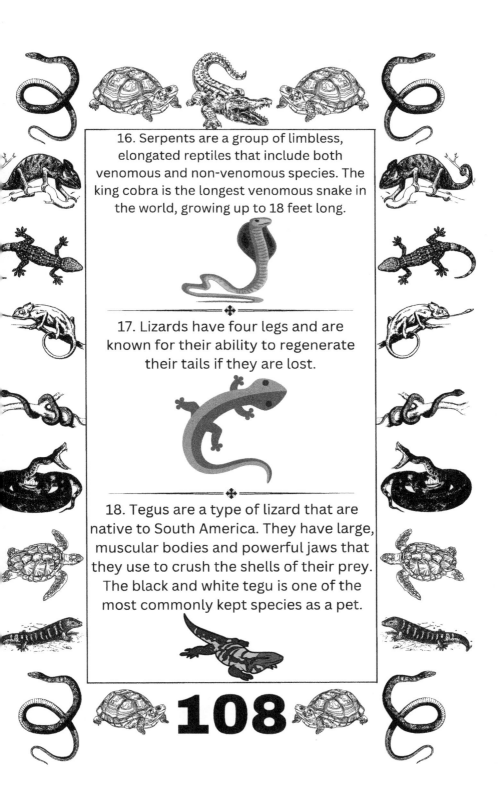

16. Serpents are a group of limbless, elongated reptiles that include both venomous and non-venomous species. The king cobra is the longest venomous snake in the world, growing up to 18 feet long.

17. Lizards have four legs and are known for their ability to regenerate their tails if they are lost.

18. Tegus are a type of lizard that are native to South America. They have large, muscular bodies and powerful jaws that they use to crush the shells of their prey. The black and white tegu is one of the most commonly kept species as a pet.

19. Alligators are a type of crocodilian that are found in the southeastern United States and China. They have broad snouts and powerful tails that they use to swim through the water.

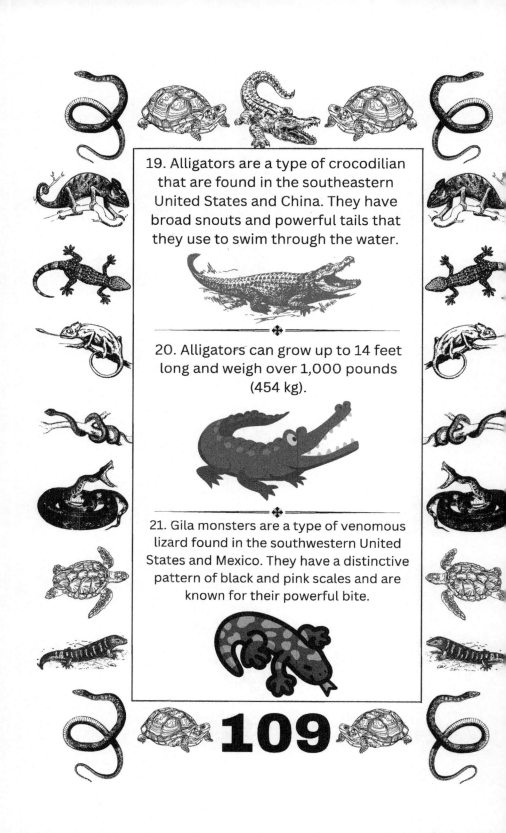

20. Alligators can grow up to 14 feet long and weigh over 1,000 pounds (454 kg).

21. Gila monsters are a type of venomous lizard found in the southwestern United States and Mexico. They have a distinctive pattern of black and pink scales and are known for their powerful bite.

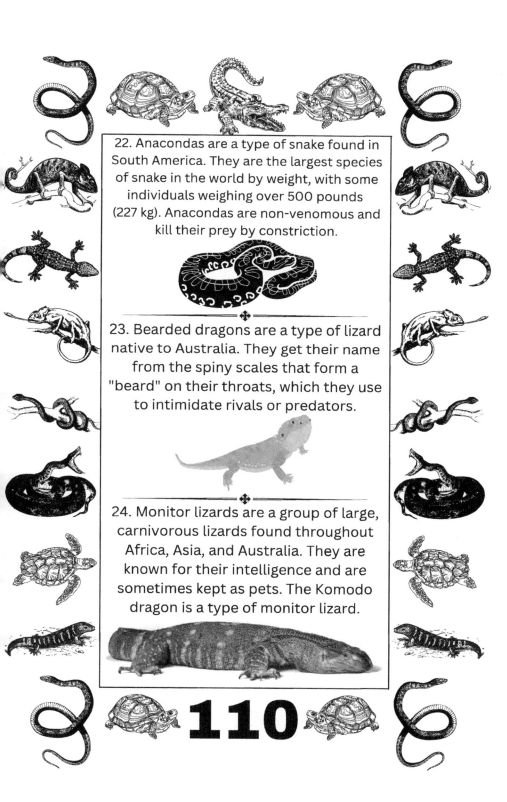

22. Anacondas are a type of snake found in South America. They are the largest species of snake in the world by weight, with some individuals weighing over 500 pounds (227 kg). Anacondas are non-venomous and kill their prey by constriction.

23. Bearded dragons are a type of lizard native to Australia. They get their name from the spiny scales that form a "beard" on their throats, which they use to intimidate rivals or predators.

24. Monitor lizards are a group of large, carnivorous lizards found throughout Africa, Asia, and Australia. They are known for their intelligence and are sometimes kept as pets. The Komodo dragon is a type of monitor lizard.

25. Horned lizards are known for their distinctive spiny appearance and their ability to shoot blood from their eyes as a defense mechanism.

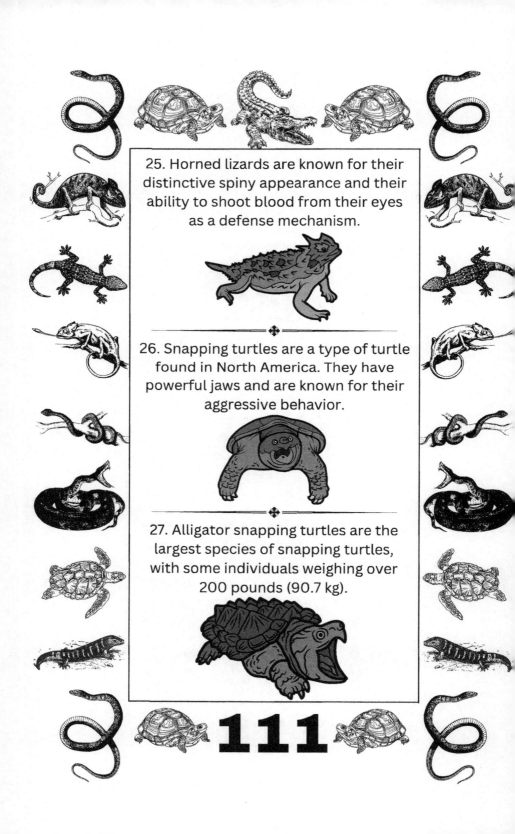

26. Snapping turtles are a type of turtle found in North America. They have powerful jaws and are known for their aggressive behavior.

27. Alligator snapping turtles are the largest species of snapping turtles, with some individuals weighing over 200 pounds (90.7 kg).

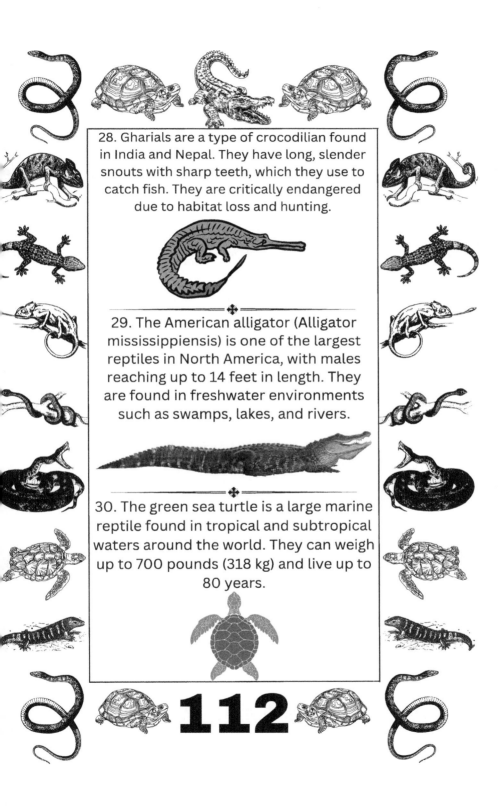

28. Gharials are a type of crocodilian found in India and Nepal. They have long, slender snouts with sharp teeth, which they use to catch fish. They are critically endangered due to habitat loss and hunting.

❖

29. The American alligator (Alligator mississippiensis) is one of the largest reptiles in North America, with males reaching up to 14 feet in length. They are found in freshwater environments such as swamps, lakes, and rivers.

❖

30. The green sea turtle is a large marine reptile found in tropical and subtropical waters around the world. They can weigh up to 700 pounds (318 kg) and live up to 80 years.

31. The Indian python is one of the largest snakes in the world, capable of reaching lengths of over 20 feet. They are found in the forests and grasslands of South Asia.

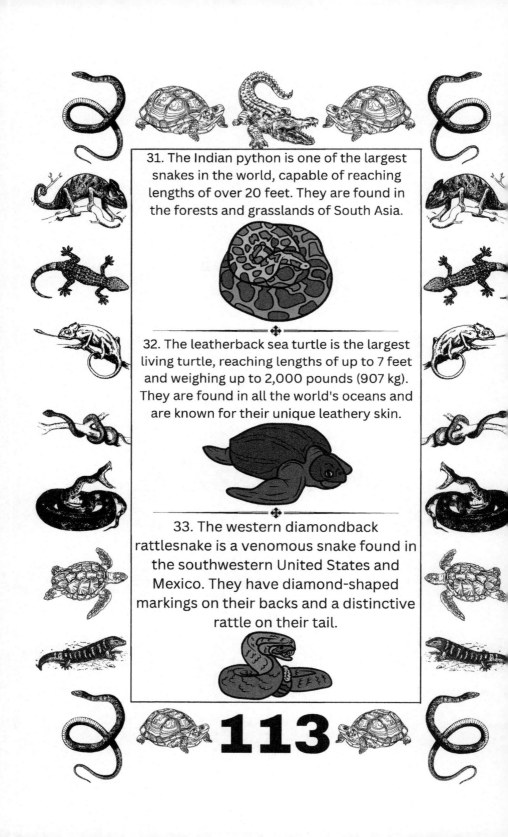

32. The leatherback sea turtle is the largest living turtle, reaching lengths of up to 7 feet and weighing up to 2,000 pounds (907 kg). They are found in all the world's oceans and are known for their unique leathery skin.

33. The western diamondback rattlesnake is a venomous snake found in the southwestern United States and Mexico. They have diamond-shaped markings on their backs and a distinctive rattle on their tail.

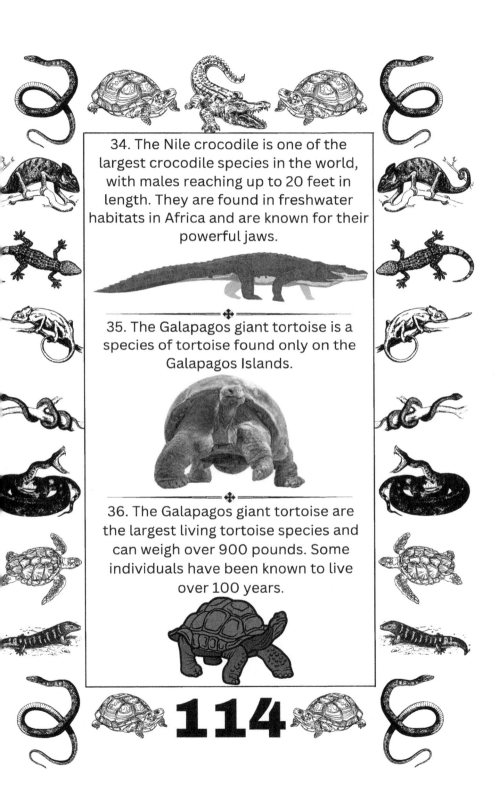

34. The Nile crocodile is one of the largest crocodile species in the world, with males reaching up to 20 feet in length. They are found in freshwater habitats in Africa and are known for their powerful jaws.

35. The Galapagos giant tortoise is a species of tortoise found only on the Galapagos Islands.

36. The Galapagos giant tortoise are the largest living tortoise species and can weigh over 900 pounds. Some individuals have been known to live over 100 years.

37. The frilled lizard is a species of lizard found in Australia and New Guinea. They are known for the frill of skin around their necks that they use to intimidate predators.

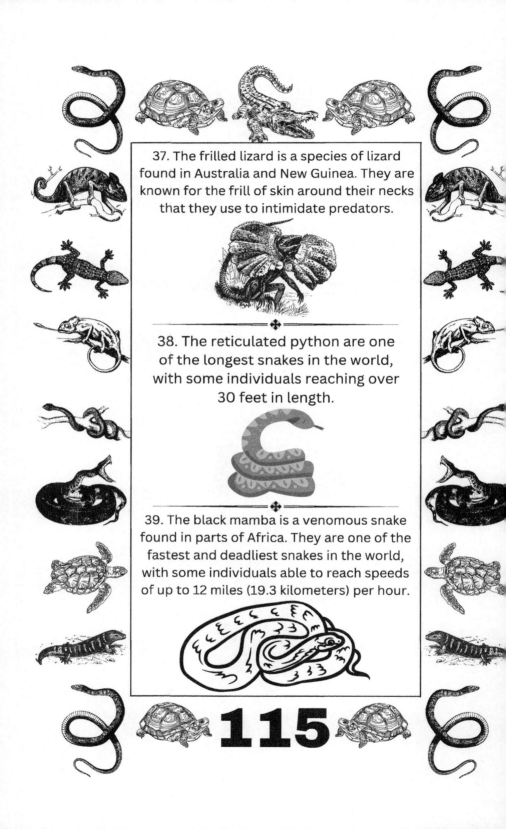

38. The reticulated python are one of the longest snakes in the world, with some individuals reaching over 30 feet in length.

39. The black mamba is a venomous snake found in parts of Africa. They are one of the fastest and deadliest snakes in the world, with some individuals able to reach speeds of up to 12 miles (19.3 kilometers) per hour.

40. The diamondback terrapin is the only species of turtle found in brackish waters along the eastern coast of North America. They are named for their diamond-shaped shell markings

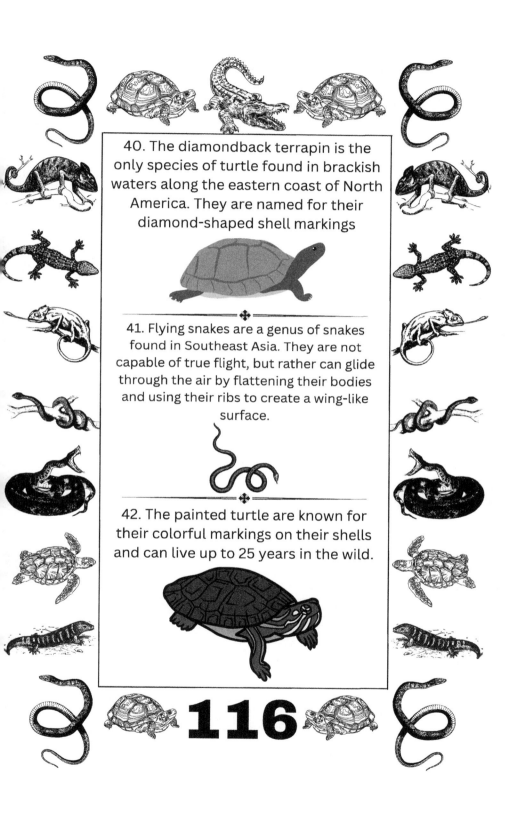

41. Flying snakes are a genus of snakes found in Southeast Asia. They are not capable of true flight, but rather can glide through the air by flattening their bodies and using their ribs to create a wing-like surface.

42. The painted turtle are known for their colorful markings on their shells and can live up to 25 years in the wild.

43. Sea snakes are a family of venomous snakes found in the oceans around the world. They are adapted to life in the water and have flattened tails for swimming.

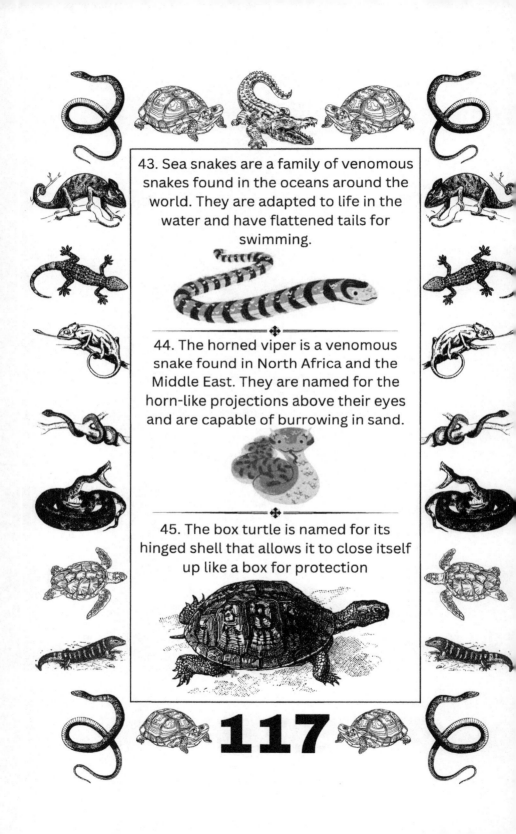

44. The horned viper is a venomous snake found in North Africa and the Middle East. They are named for the horn-like projections above their eyes and are capable of burrowing in sand.

45. The box turtle is named for its hinged shell that allows it to close itself up like a box for protection

46. Basilisk lizards are a genus of lizards found in Central and South America. They are also known as "Jesus lizards" because of their ability to run across the surface of water.

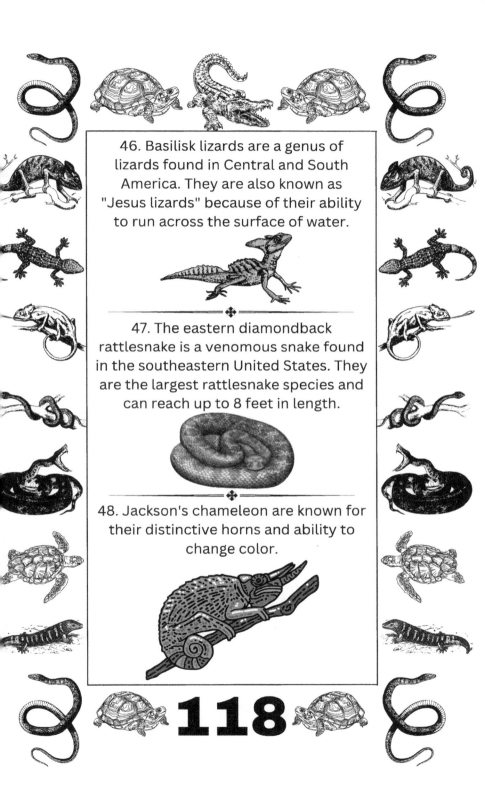

47. The eastern diamondback rattlesnake is a venomous snake found in the southeastern United States. They are the largest rattlesnake species and can reach up to 8 feet in length.

48. Jackson's chameleon are known for their distinctive horns and ability to change color.

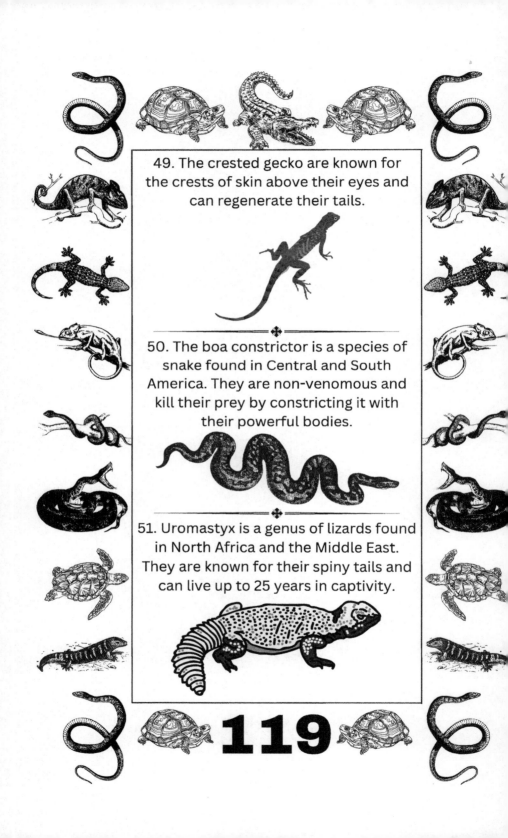

49. The crested gecko are known for the crests of skin above their eyes and can regenerate their tails.

50. The boa constrictor is a species of snake found in Central and South America. They are non-venomous and kill their prey by constricting it with their powerful bodies.

51. Uromastyx is a genus of lizards found in North Africa and the Middle East. They are known for their spiny tails and can live up to 25 years in captivity.

52. The Madagascar day gecko is a species of gecko found in Madagascar. They are brightly colored and have distinctive large eyes.

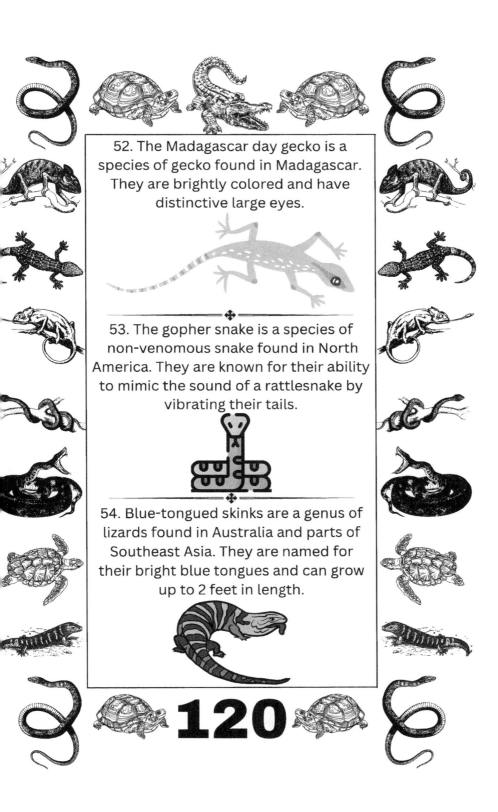

53. The gopher snake is a species of non-venomous snake found in North America. They are known for their ability to mimic the sound of a rattlesnake by vibrating their tails.

54. Blue-tongued skinks are a genus of lizards found in Australia and parts of Southeast Asia. They are named for their bright blue tongues and can grow up to 2 feet in length.

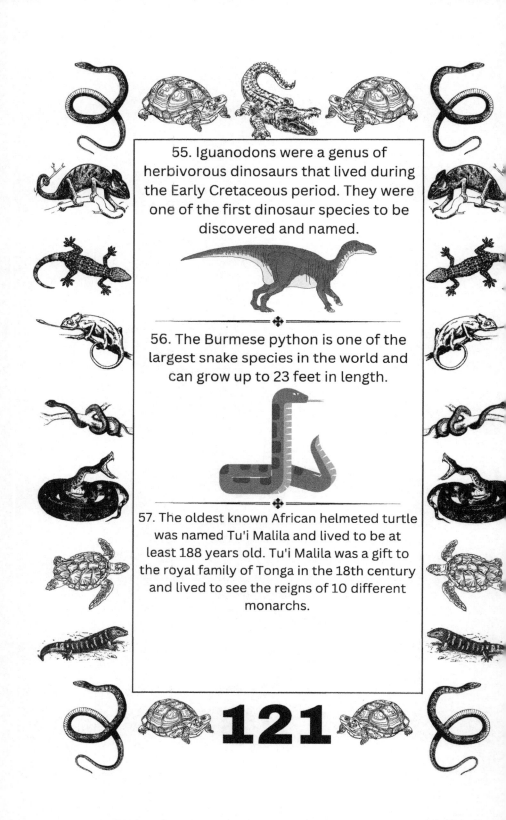

55. Iguanodons were a genus of herbivorous dinosaurs that lived during the Early Cretaceous period. They were one of the first dinosaur species to be discovered and named.

56. The Burmese python is one of the largest snake species in the world and can grow up to 23 feet in length.

57. The oldest known African helmeted turtle was named Tu'i Malila and lived to be at least 188 years old. Tu'i Malila was a gift to the royal family of Tonga in the 18th century and lived to see the reigns of 10 different monarchs.

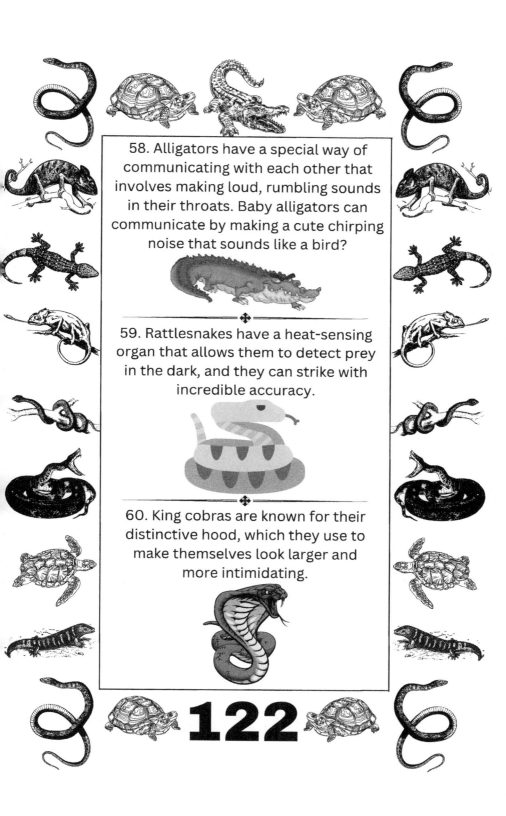

58. Alligators have a special way of communicating with each other that involves making loud, rumbling sounds in their throats. Baby alligators can communicate by making a cute chirping noise that sounds like a bird?

59. Rattlesnakes have a heat-sensing organ that allows them to detect prey in the dark, and they can strike with incredible accuracy.

60. King cobras are known for their distinctive hood, which they use to make themselves look larger and more intimidating.

61. Anacondas are known for their ability to constrict their prey, squeezing them to death before swallowing them whole.

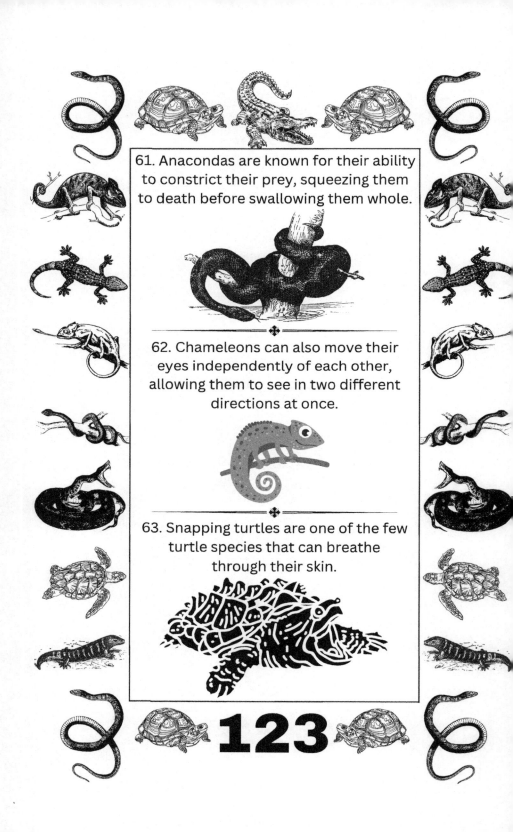

62. Chameleons can also move their eyes independently of each other, allowing them to see in two different directions at once.

63. Snapping turtles are one of the few turtle species that can breathe through their skin.

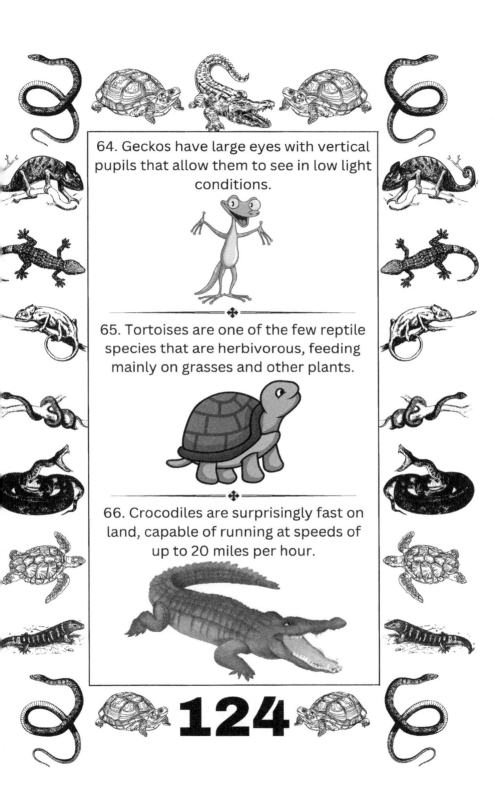

64. Geckos have large eyes with vertical pupils that allow them to see in low light conditions.

65. Tortoises are one of the few reptile species that are herbivorous, feeding mainly on grasses and other plants.

66. Crocodiles are surprisingly fast on land, capable of running at speeds of up to 20 miles per hour.

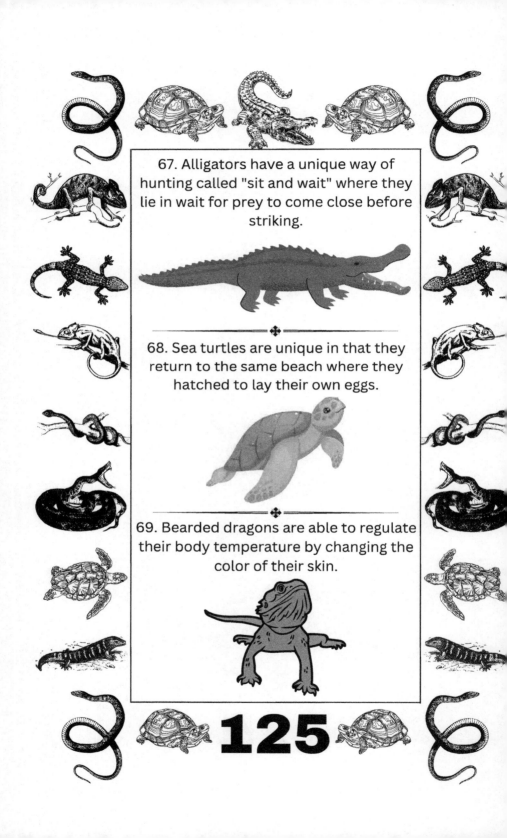

67. Alligators have a unique way of hunting called "sit and wait" where they lie in wait for prey to come close before striking.

68. Sea turtles are unique in that they return to the same beach where they hatched to lay their own eggs.

69. Bearded dragons are able to regulate their body temperature by changing the color of their skin.

70. Boa constrictors can eat prey that is much larger than their own head due to their ability to dislocate their jaw.

71. Green anoles are lizards that are native to the southeastern United States and are known for their ability to change color based on their mood and surroundings.

72. Green anoles are able to detach their tails as a defense mechanism.

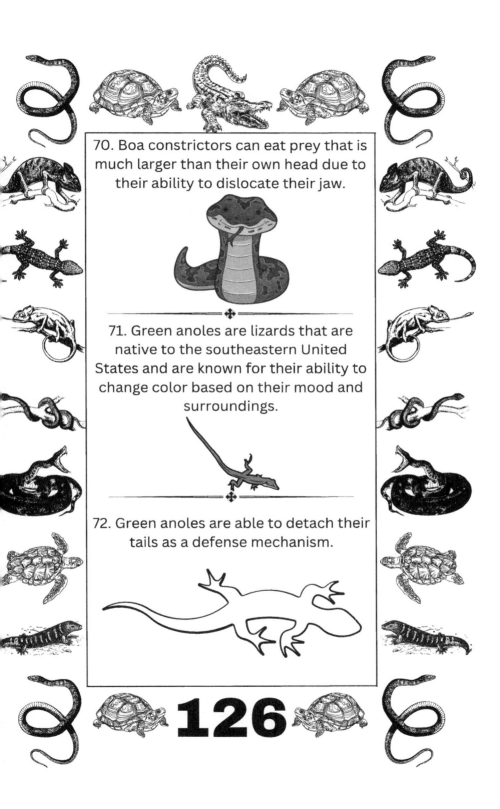

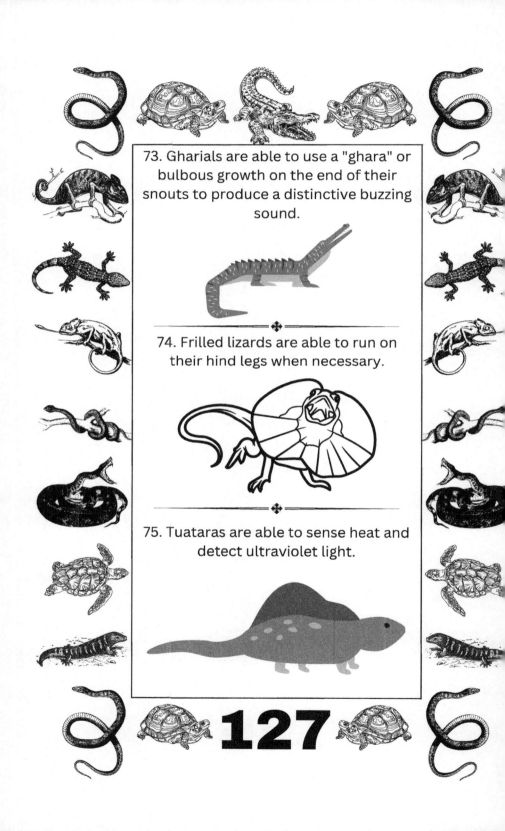

73. Gharials are able to use a "ghara" or bulbous growth on the end of their snouts to produce a distinctive buzzing sound.

74. Frilled lizards are able to run on their hind legs when necessary.

75. Tuataras are able to sense heat and detect ultraviolet light.

76. Gaboon vipers are venomous snakes that are found in Africa and are known for their extremely long fangs, which can measure up to two inches in length.

77. Gaboon vipers are also able to camouflage themselves extremely well with their unique, triangular-shaped heads.

78. Iridescent skinks are lizards that are found in New Zealand and are named for their shimmering, iridescent scales. They are also able to shed their tails as a defense mechanism.

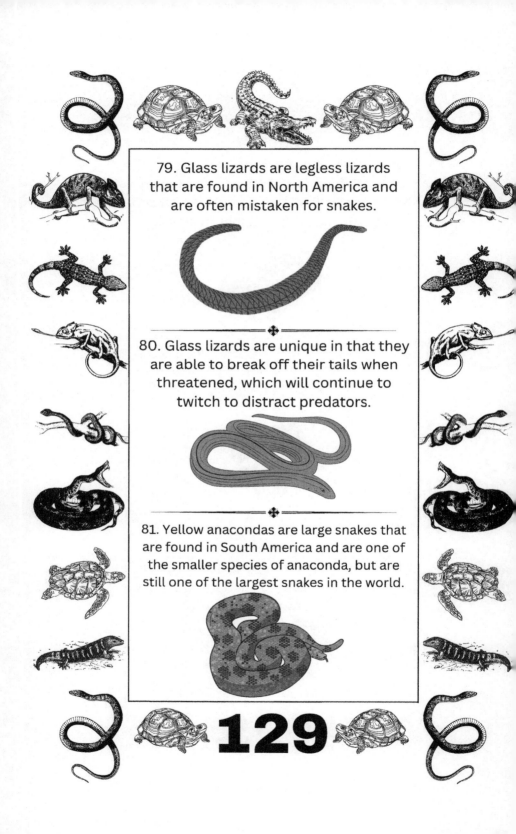

79. Glass lizards are legless lizards that are found in North America and are often mistaken for snakes.

80. Glass lizards are unique in that they are able to break off their tails when threatened, which will continue to twitch to distract predators.

81. Yellow anacondas are large snakes that are found in South America and are one of the smaller species of anaconda, but are still one of the largest snakes in the world.

82. Burmese pythons are able to eat extremely large prey, including alligators, and can go for long periods of time without eating.

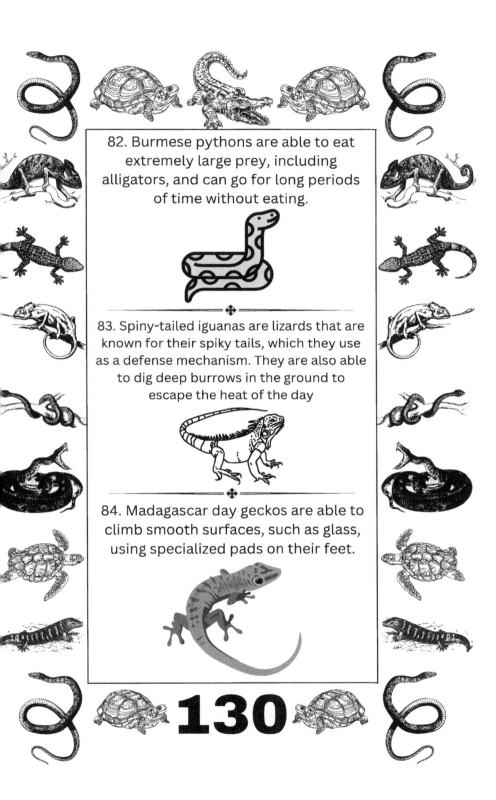

83. Spiny-tailed iguanas are lizards that are known for their spiky tails, which they use as a defense mechanism. They are also able to dig deep burrows in the ground to escape the heat of the day

84. Madagascar day geckos are able to climb smooth surfaces, such as glass, using specialized pads on their feet.

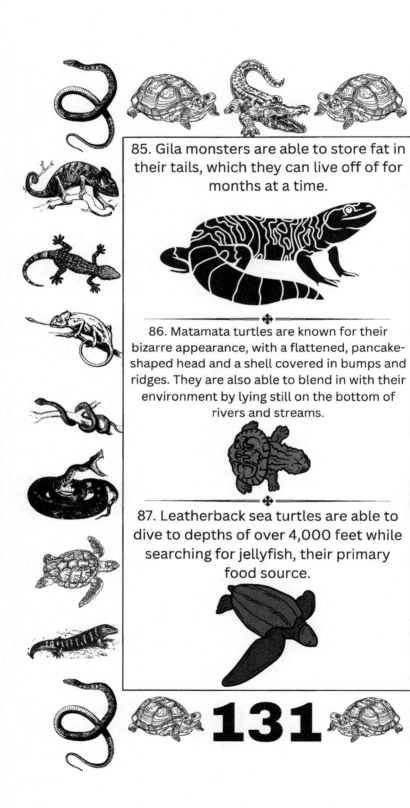

85. Gila monsters are able to store fat in their tails, which they can live off of for months at a time.

86. Matamata turtles are known for their bizarre appearance, with a flattened, pancake-shaped head and a shell covered in bumps and ridges. They are also able to blend in with their environment by lying still on the bottom of rivers and streams.

87. Leatherback sea turtles are able to dive to depths of over 4,000 feet while searching for jellyfish, their primary food source.

131

88. Emerald tree boas are non-venomous snakes that are found in South America and are known for their striking emerald green coloration.

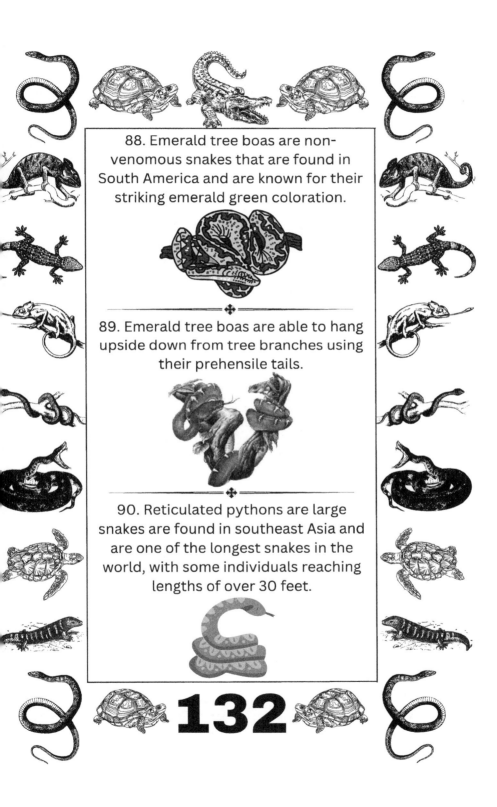

89. Emerald tree boas are able to hang upside down from tree branches using their prehensile tails.

90. Reticulated pythons are large snakes are found in southeast Asia and are one of the longest snakes in the world, with some individuals reaching lengths of over 30 feet.

91. Reticulated pythons are able to eat large prey, including deer and pigs.

92. Hognose snakes have a unique ability to play dead when threatened, flipping over onto their back and sticking out their tongue as if they are dead.

93. Mallee dragons are a species of lizard found in Australia that have a unique behavior where they climb trees and bask in the sun during the day, and retreat to their underground burrows at night.

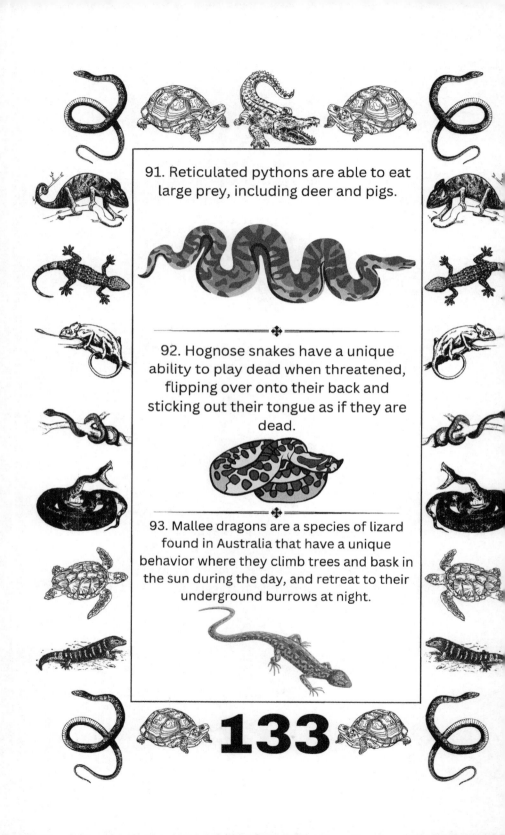

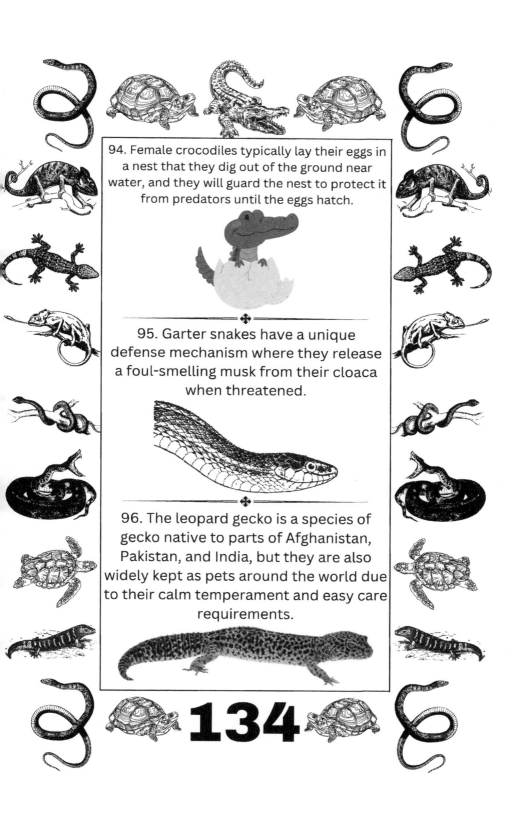

94. Female crocodiles typically lay their eggs in a nest that they dig out of the ground near water, and they will guard the nest to protect it from predators until the eggs hatch.

95. Garter snakes have a unique defense mechanism where they release a foul-smelling musk from their cloaca when threatened.

96. The leopard gecko is a species of gecko native to parts of Afghanistan, Pakistan, and India, but they are also widely kept as pets around the world due to their calm temperament and easy care requirements.

134

97. Leopard geckos are named for their spotted pattern, which resembles the fur of a leopard.
Unlike many other gecko species, leopard geckos have movable eyelids, which they use to blink.

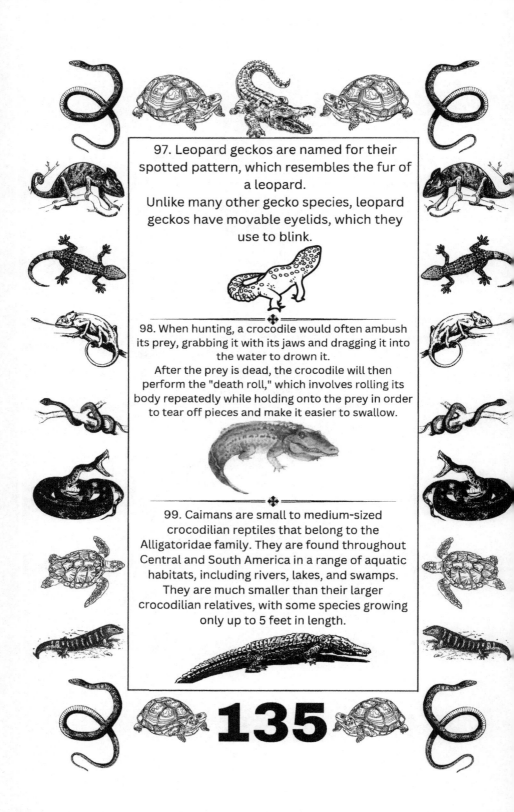

98. When hunting, a crocodile would often ambush its prey, grabbing it with its jaws and dragging it into the water to drown it.
After the prey is dead, the crocodile will then perform the "death roll," which involves rolling its body repeatedly while holding onto the prey in order to tear off pieces and make it easier to swallow.

99. Caimans are small to medium-sized crocodilian reptiles that belong to the Alligatoridae family. They are found throughout Central and South America in a range of aquatic habitats, including rivers, lakes, and swamps.
They are much smaller than their larger crocodilian relatives, with some species growing only up to 5 feet in length.

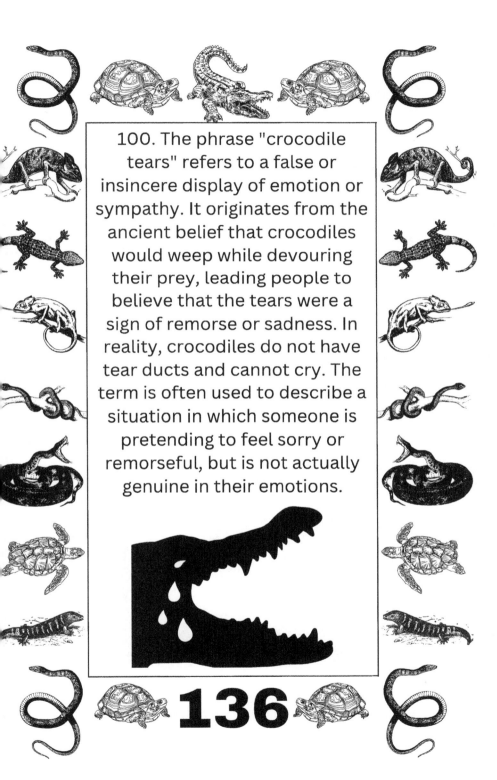

100. The phrase "crocodile tears" refers to a false or insincere display of emotion or sympathy. It originates from the ancient belief that crocodiles would weep while devouring their prey, leading people to believe that the tears were a sign of remorse or sadness. In reality, crocodiles do not have tear ducts and cannot cry. The term is often used to describe a situation in which someone is pretending to feel sorry or remorseful, but is not actually genuine in their emotions.

136

5- Amphibians

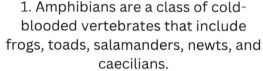

1. Amphibians are a class of cold-blooded vertebrates that include frogs, toads, salamanders, newts, and caecilians.
They are found in a variety of habitats, including forests, deserts, freshwater and saltwater ecosystems, and even underground.

---

2. Amphibians have a unique life cycle that includes metamorphosis, where they hatch from eggs as aquatic larvae with gills and then transform into terrestrial adults with lungs.
Most amphibians breathe through their skin, which must remain moist for oxygen to diffuse into their bloodstream. This is why they are often found near water.

---

3. There are over 8,000 known species of amphibians. Amphibians have been around for a very long time, with the earliest known amphibian-like creatures dating back over 370 million years to the late Devonian period.

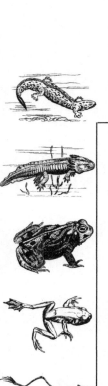

4. The largest amphibian in the world is the Chinese giant salamander, which can grow up to six feet long and weigh over 100 pounds.

5. The smallest amphibian in the world is the Paedophryne Amauensis, a frog that is found in Papua New Guinea and measures less than 0.3 inches long.

6. Some amphibians, such as poison dart frogs, have brightly colored skin that warns predators that they are toxic and should not be eaten.

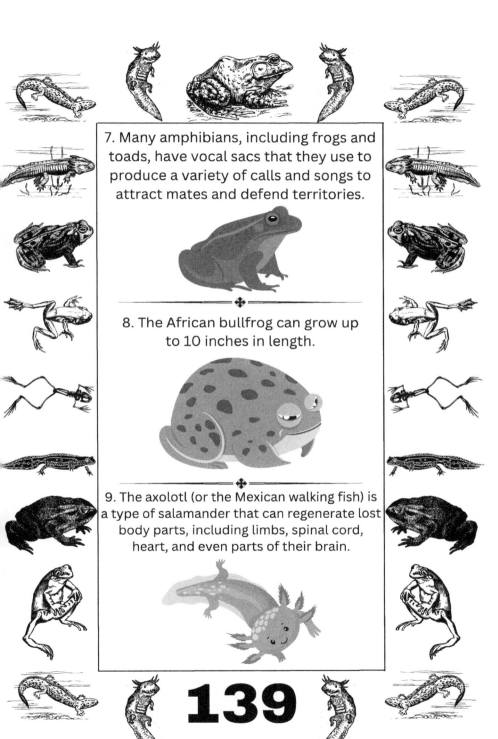

7. Many amphibians, including frogs and toads, have vocal sacs that they use to produce a variety of calls and songs to attract mates and defend territories.

8. The African bullfrog can grow up to 10 inches in length.

9. The axolotl (or the Mexican walking fish) is a type of salamander that can regenerate lost body parts, including limbs, spinal cord, heart, and even parts of their brain.

10. The poison dart frog is one of the most brightly colored amphibians in the world.

11. The cane toad is native to South and Central America but has been introduced to other countries.

12. The common frog can breathe through its skin as well as its lungs.

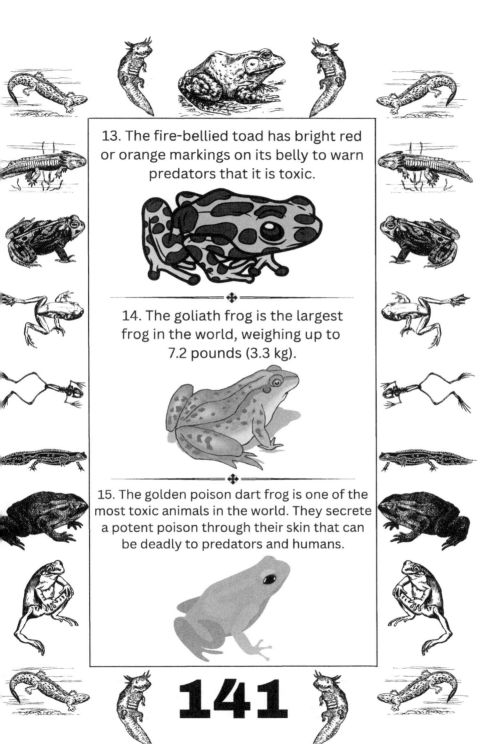

13. The fire-bellied toad has bright red or orange markings on its belly to warn predators that it is toxic.

14. The goliath frog is the largest frog in the world, weighing up to 7.2 pounds (3.3 kg).

15. The golden poison dart frog is one of the most toxic animals in the world. They secrete a potent poison through their skin that can be deadly to predators and humans.

16. The hellbender salamander is found only in eastern North America and can live up to 30 years.

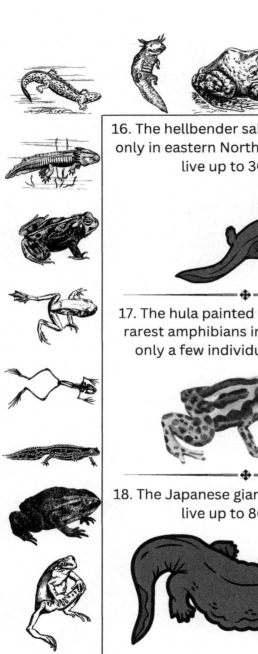

---

17. The hula painted frog is one of the rarest amphibians in the world, with only a few individuals remaining.

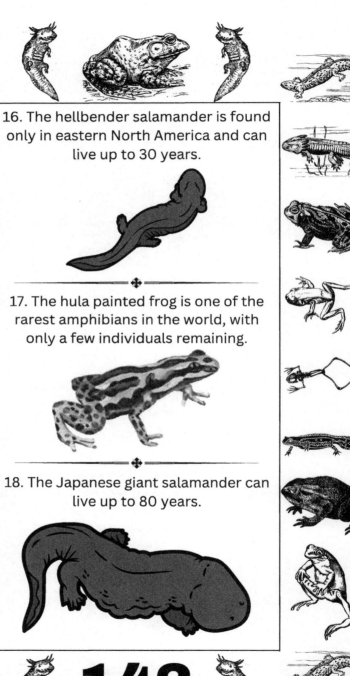

---

18. The Japanese giant salamander can live up to 80 years.

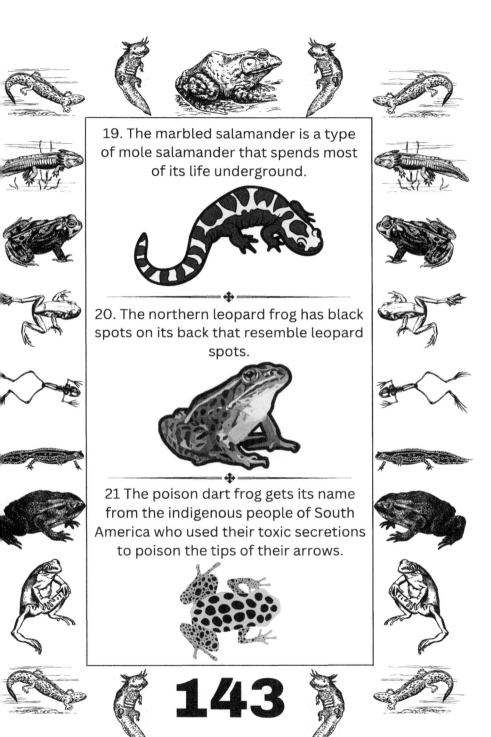

19. The marbled salamander is a type of mole salamander that spends most of its life underground.

20. The northern leopard frog has black spots on its back that resemble leopard spots.

21 The poison dart frog gets its name from the indigenous people of South America who used their toxic secretions to poison the tips of their arrows.

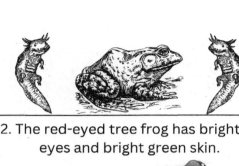

22. The red-eyed tree frog has bright red eyes and bright green skin.

23. The saddleback toad gets its name from the saddle-shaped marking on its back.

24. The spotted salamander has yellow spots on its black skin.

144

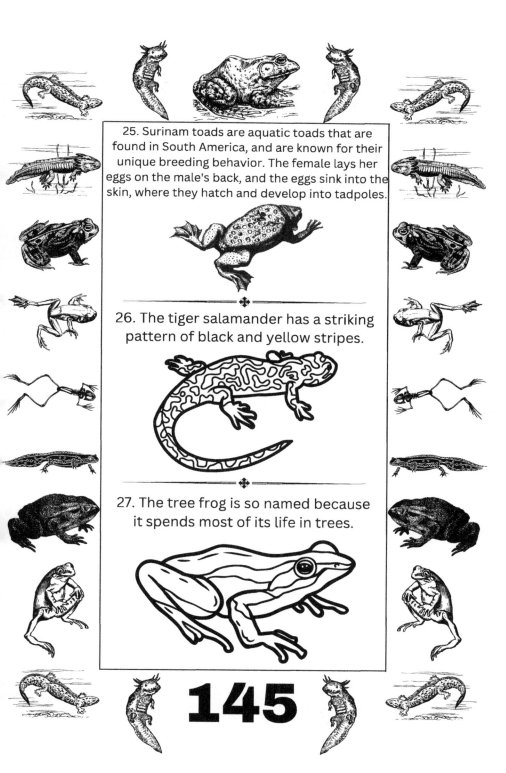

25. Surinam toads are aquatic toads that are found in South America, and are known for their unique breeding behavior. The female lays her eggs on the male's back, and the eggs sink into the skin, where they hatch and develop into tadpoles.

26. The tiger salamander has a striking pattern of black and yellow stripes.

27. The tree frog is so named because it spends most of its life in trees.

145

28. The waxy monkey tree frog secretes a waxy substance that protects its skin from drying out.

29. The American bullfrog is the largest frog in North America.

30. The barking tree frog has a loud, dog-like bark.

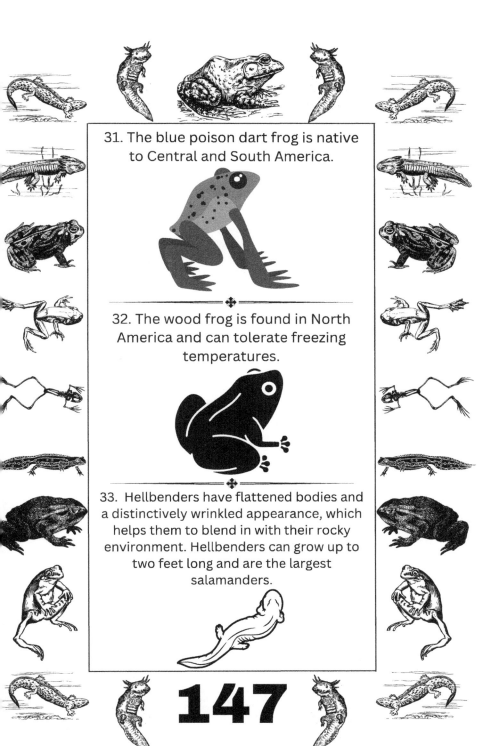

31. The blue poison dart frog is native to Central and South America.

32. The wood frog is found in North America and can tolerate freezing temperatures.

33. Hellbenders have flattened bodies and a distinctively wrinkled appearance, which helps them to blend in with their rocky environment. Hellbenders can grow up to two feet long and are the largest salamanders.

147

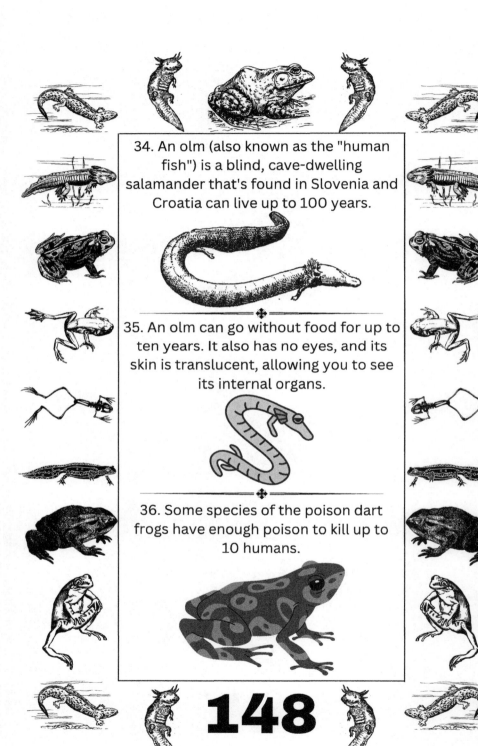

34. An olm (also known as the "human fish") is a blind, cave-dwelling salamander that's found in Slovenia and Croatia can live up to 100 years.

35. An olm can go without food for up to ten years. It also has no eyes, and its skin is translucent, allowing you to see its internal organs.

36. Some species of the poison dart frogs have enough poison to kill up to 10 humans.

37. Glass frogs have transparent skin on their underside, allowing you to see their internal organs.

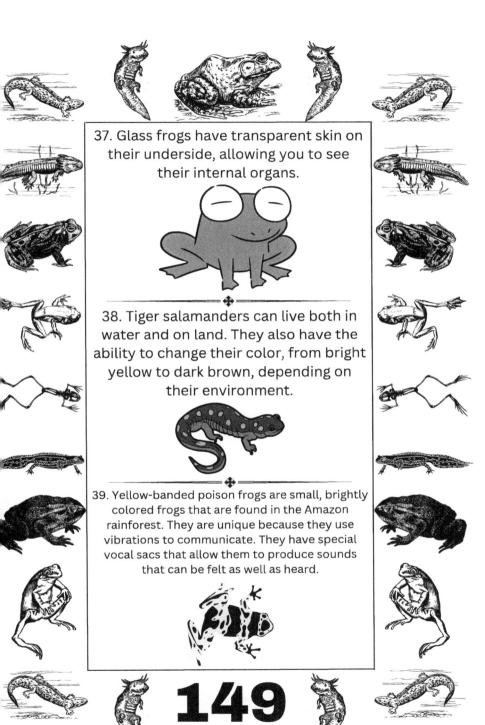

38. Tiger salamanders can live both in water and on land. They also have the ability to change their color, from bright yellow to dark brown, depending on their environment.

39. Yellow-banded poison frogs are small, brightly colored frogs that are found in the Amazon rainforest. They are unique because they use vibrations to communicate. They have special vocal sacs that allow them to produce sounds that can be felt as well as heard.

40. African clawed frogs are fully aquatic frogs that are found in Sub-Saharan Africa. They have no tongue and catch prey by using their strong jaws and front legs to push food into their mouths.

---

41. African clawed frogs are used extensively in medical research, as they are very resilient and can regenerate damaged tissues.

---

42. Suriname horned frogs are large and terrestrial frogs that are found in South America and are known for their unusual appearance. They have a fleshy horn-like protrusion above each eye, which they use to intimidate predators.

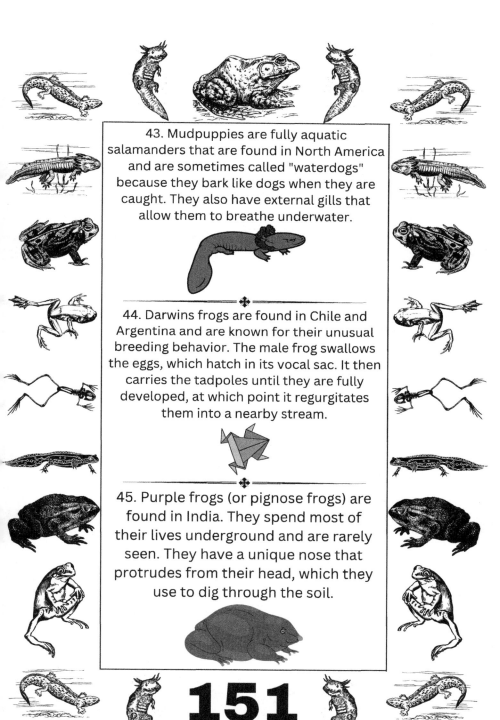

43. Mudpuppies are fully aquatic salamanders that are found in North America and are sometimes called "waterdogs" because they bark like dogs when they are caught. They also have external gills that allow them to breathe underwater.

44. Darwins frogs are found in Chile and Argentina and are known for their unusual breeding behavior. The male frog swallows the eggs, which hatch in its vocal sac. It then carries the tadpoles until they are fully developed, at which point it regurgitates them into a nearby stream.

45. Purple frogs (or pignose frogs) are found in India. They spend most of their lives underground and are rarely seen. They have a unique nose that protrudes from their head, which they use to dig through the soil.

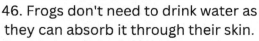

46. Frogs don't need to drink water as they can absorb it through their skin.

❖

47. The term "frog" is often used to refer to all amphibians, but technically, only members of the order Anura are true frogs.

❖

48. Frogs use their eyes to help them swallow their prey, as they push their eyeballs down into their mouths to help push the food down their throats.

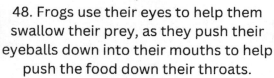

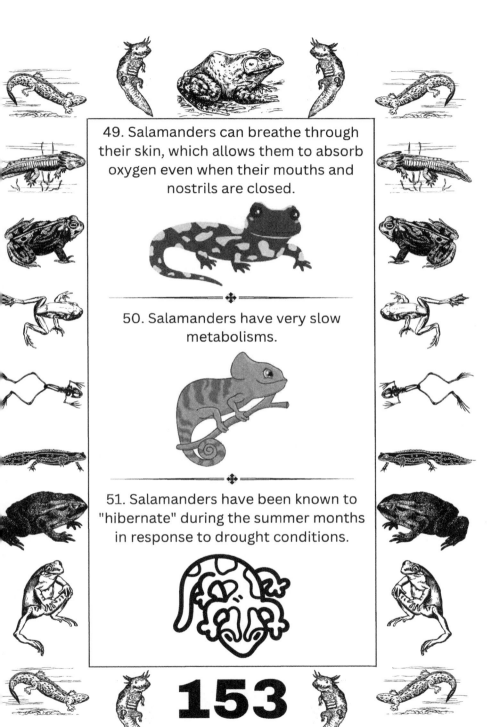

49. Salamanders can breathe through their skin, which allows them to absorb oxygen even when their mouths and nostrils are closed.

50. Salamanders have very slow metabolisms.

51. Salamanders have been known to "hibernate" during the summer months in response to drought conditions.

153

52. Axolotls have no eyelids and have a permanent smile on their faces, giving them a perpetually happy appearance.

✤

53. Axolotls are excellent swimmers and can use their long tails to propel themselves through the water with ease.

✤

54. Axolotls are not a threatened species, but their natural habitat is threatened by pollution and development.

55. Unlike most salamanders, newts are semi-aquatic, spending part of their time in water and part of their time on land.

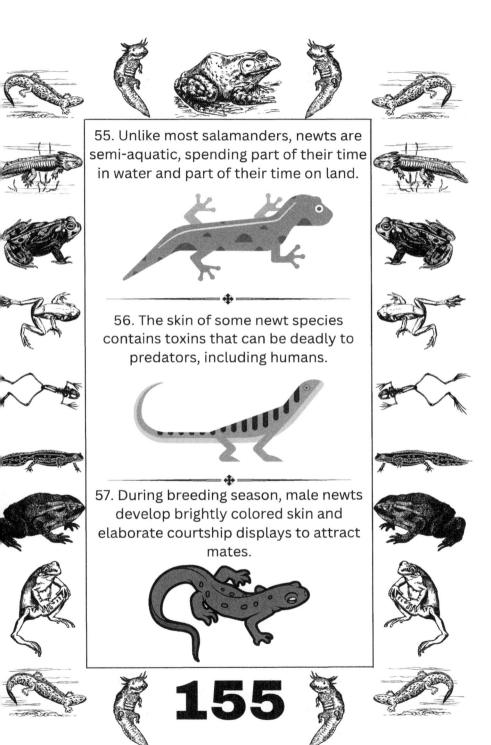

56. The skin of some newt species contains toxins that can be deadly to predators, including humans.

57. During breeding season, male newts develop brightly colored skin and elaborate courtship displays to attract mates.

58. Newts have a unique life cycle, with many species undergoing metamorphosis from a fully aquatic larva to a terrestrial adult.

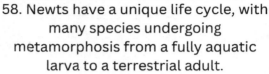

59. Newts have a long lifespan compared to other amphibians, with some species living for up to 30 years in the wild.

60. Some species of newts, such as the great crested newt, are protected by law in many countries due to habitat loss and other threats. Newts are popular pets, but it is important to ensure that they are obtained legally and that their care requirements are met, including providing a suitable habitat and diet.

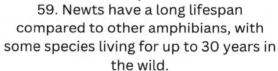

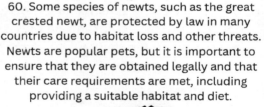

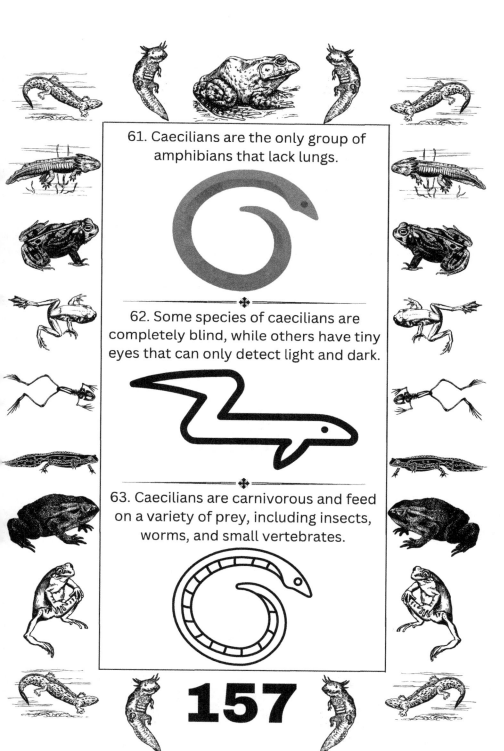

61. Caecilians are the only group of amphibians that lack lungs.

62. Some species of caecilians are completely blind, while others have tiny eyes that can only detect light and dark.

63. Caecilians are carnivorous and feed on a variety of prey, including insects, worms, and small vertebrates.

157

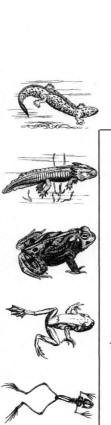

64. Caecilians are important decomposers in many ecosystems, helping to break down dead plant and animal material.

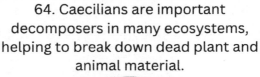

65. Because they spend most of their time underground, caecilians are rarely seen by humans and are poorly understood compared to other amphibian groups.

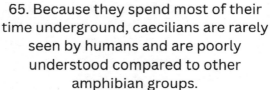

66. The largest species of caecilian is the giant caecilian, which can grow up to 5 feet (1.5 meters) long.

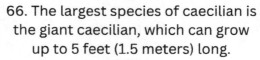

67. Toads are a type of amphibian that are closely related to frogs, but have dry, warty skin and shorter legs.

68. Toads hibernate during the winter months to conserve energy and avoid the cold.

69. Toads lay their eggs in long strings, with the eggs hatching into tadpoles that eventually metamorphose into adult toads.

159

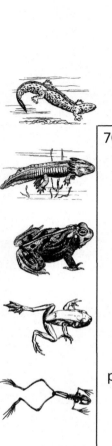

70. The most common species of toad in North America is the American toad, which is known for its distinctive "trilling" call.

---

71. Giant waxy monkey tree frogs are unique because they have a waxy substance on their skin that helps protect them from dehydration in their arid environment.

---

72. Eastern spadefoot toads are unique because they have a hard, spade-like structure on their hind legs that they use to burrow underground.

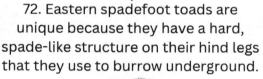

73. Alpine newts are unique because they have the ability to change their skin color to blend in with their environment, and males develop bright orange bellies during the breeding season to attract females.

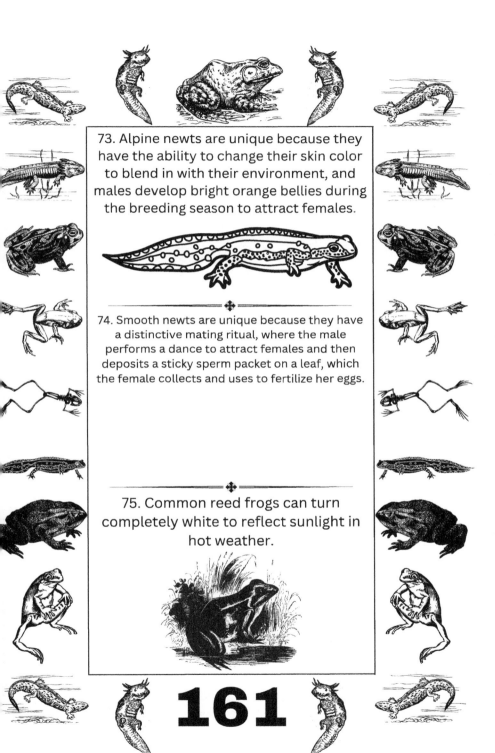

74. Smooth newts are unique because they have a distinctive mating ritual, where the male performs a dance to attract females and then deposits a sticky sperm packet on a leaf, which the female collects and uses to fertilize her eggs.

75. Common reed frogs can turn completely white to reflect sunlight in hot weather.

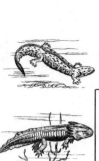

76. Black salamanders are unique because they are completely black, and they are able to lay their eggs on land instead of in water.

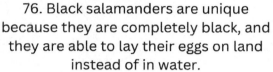

77. Anderson's salamander, also known as the Black Warrior Waterdog, is a large, fully aquatic salamander found in the southeastern United States, specifically in Alabama, Georgia, and Tennessee.

78. Horned frogs are known for their large mouth and aggressive feeding behavior, which has earned them the nickname "Pacman frog". Pacman frogs are primarily terrestrial and are often kept as pets.

79. The Puerto Rican crested toad is a species of toad found only in Puerto Rico. They are listed as an endangered species due to habitat loss and the spread of a fungal disease known as chytridiomycosis.

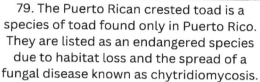

80. Gray tree frogs are known for their ability to change color from gray to green depending on their surroundings. They are primarily arboreal and are often found in wooded habitats.

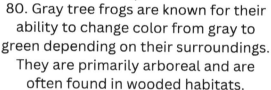

81. The purple frog is also considered a "living fossil," as it belongs to a group of frogs that evolved over 130 million years ago and has remained relatively unchanged since then.

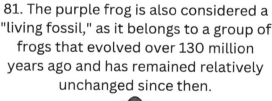

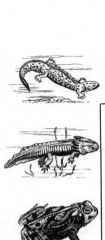

82. Frog eggs are typically laid in clusters or masses, and can contain anywhere from a few dozen to several thousand eggs, depending on the species.

The outer layer of a frog egg is a gelatinous material that helps to protect the developing embryo from predators and other threats.

Frog eggs are usually attached to vegetation or other structures in or near the water, where they will develop into tadpoles. Tadpoles develop from the fertilized eggs and undergo a metamorphosis into juvenile frogs.

83. Male common frogs can be distinguished from females by their swollen thumbs, which are used during mating to grip onto the female's back.

84. Common frogs are also known as garden frogs. They hibernate during winter, often burrowing into mud or leaf litter at the bottom of ponds or other bodies of water.

85. In some parts of the world, including India and Australia, there have been reports of rain that is accompanied by falling frogs. This phenomenon is known as "frog rain" and is believed to occur when strong winds or tornadoes pick up large groups of frogs from bodies of water and carry them through the air, dropping them in other locations.

86. There are more than 170 species of poison dart frogs, and they range in size from about half an inch to two and a half inches long.

87. Despite their toxic reputation, poison dart frogs are not aggressive and will usually only use their toxins as a last resort when threatened. If left alone, they are not dangerous to humans.

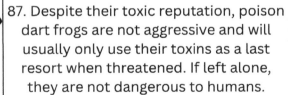

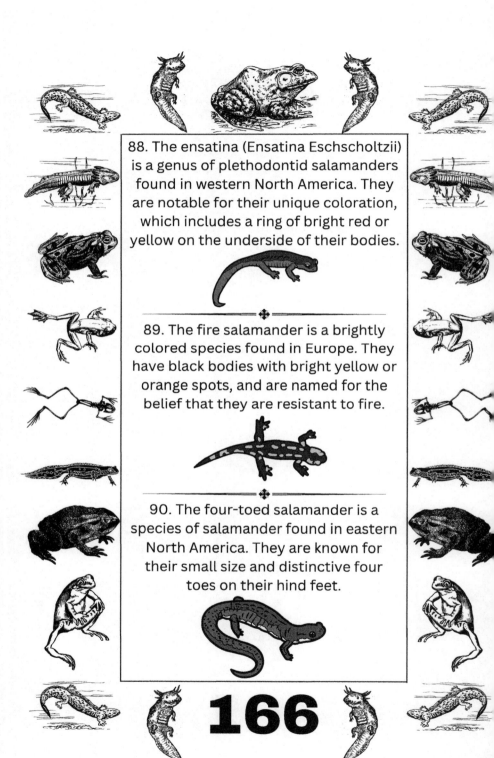

88. The ensatina (Ensatina Eschscholtzii) is a genus of plethodontid salamanders found in western North America. They are notable for their unique coloration, which includes a ring of bright red or yellow on the underside of their bodies.

89. The fire salamander is a brightly colored species found in Europe. They have black bodies with bright yellow or orange spots, and are named for the belief that they are resistant to fire.

90. The four-toed salamander is a species of salamander found in eastern North America. They are known for their small size and distinctive four toes on their hind feet.

91. The axolotl is native to the Xochimilco and Chalco regions of Mexico and can be found in freshwater lakes and canals.

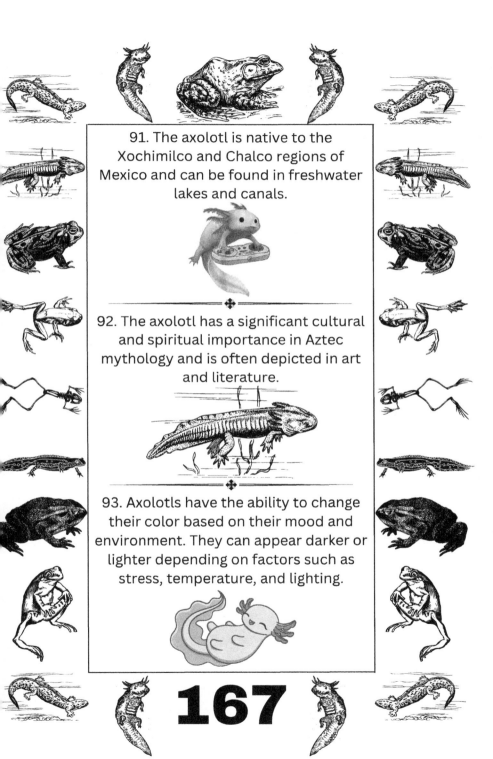

92. The axolotl has a significant cultural and spiritual importance in Aztec mythology and is often depicted in art and literature.

93. Axolotls have the ability to change their color based on their mood and environment. They can appear darker or lighter depending on factors such as stress, temperature, and lighting.

94. The axolotl is often referred to as the "Peter Pan" of salamanders because it retains its juvenile characteristics into adulthood. It's like they never grow up.

---

95. The tomato frog, found in Madagascar, secretes a sticky, milky substance from its skin when threatened.

---

96. American bullfrogs have a distinctive green or brown coloration and a loud, deep call that sounds like "jug-o-rum".

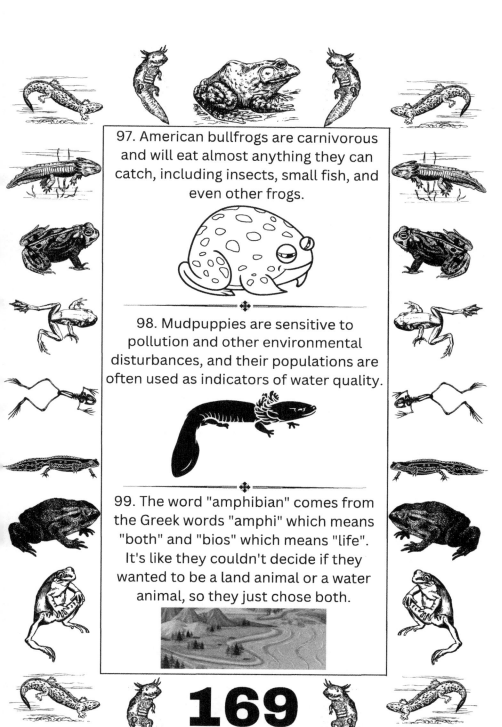

97. American bullfrogs are carnivorous and will eat almost anything they can catch, including insects, small fish, and even other frogs.

98. Mudpuppies are sensitive to pollution and other environmental disturbances, and their populations are often used as indicators of water quality.

99. The word "amphibian" comes from the Greek words "amphi" which means "both" and "bios" which means "life". It's like they couldn't decide if they wanted to be a land animal or a water animal, so they just chose both.

169

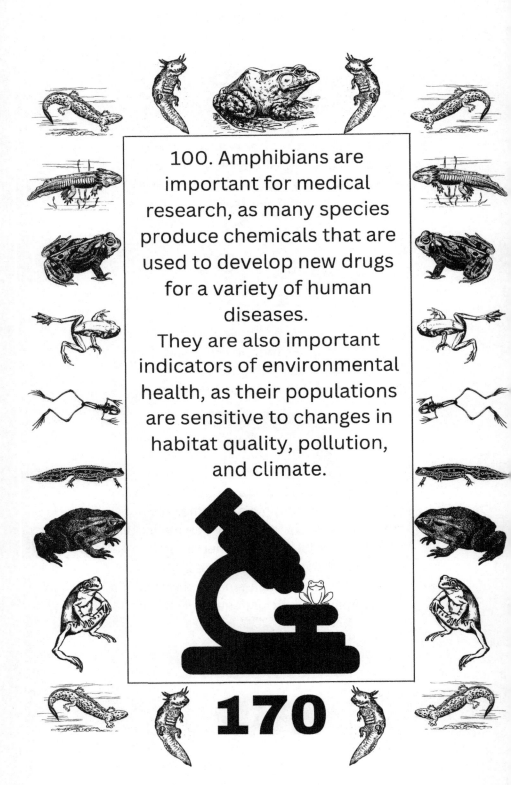

100. Amphibians are important for medical research, as many species produce chemicals that are used to develop new drugs for a variety of human diseases.
They are also important indicators of environmental health, as their populations are sensitive to changes in habitat quality, pollution, and climate.

170

Notes:

Notes:

Notes:

Printed in Great Britain
by Amazon

32539893R00106